CYBERSURFERS
& Other
Online Types

VGM Careers for You Series

CAREERS FOR

CYBERSURFERS
& Other
Online Types

Marjorie Eberts
Rachel Kelsey

VGM Career Horizons
NTC/Contemporary Publishing Company

Library of Congress Cataloging-in-Publication Data

Eberts, Marjorie.
    Careers for cybersurfers and other online types / Marjorie Eberts, Rachel
Kelsey.
        p. cm. --
    Includes bibliographical references.
    ISBN 0-8442-2296-8 (hard). -- ISBN 0-8442-2297-6 (soft)
    1. Telecommunication--Vocational guidance. 2. Internet (Computer
network)--Vocational guidance. I. Kelsey, Rachel. II. Title. III. Series.
    TK5102.6.E24   1997
    004.67'8'023--dc21   97-17555
                                                                              CIP

Published by VGM Career Horizons
An imprint of NTC/Contemporary Publishing Company
4255 West Touhy Avenue, Lincolnwood (Chicago), Illinois 60646-1975 U.S.A.
Copyright © 1998 by Marjorie Eberts and Rachel Kelsey
Manufactured in the United States of America.
International Standard Book Number: 0-8442-2296-8 (cloth)
                                                        0-8442-2297-6 (paper)
15   14   13   12   11   10   9   8   7   6   5   4   3   2   1

To Mary and Jane who introduced us to the Internet world. Thank you for keeping in touch with your daily e-mail messages.

Contents

About the Authors

M arjorie Eberts has written more than sixty books. This is her eighteenth VGM career book and her third book on careers associated with computers. She also has a syndicated newspaper column, "Dear Teacher," which appears in newspapers throughout the country. This is Rachel Kelsey's first career book. She has extensive experience with computers, especially in word processing and the construction of spreadsheets, and has written several software programs. Both Eberts and Kelsey are graduates of Stanford University.

Writing this book was a special pleasure for the authors, as it gave them the opportunity to spend hours online every day surfing the Net. They have visited every Web site mentioned in this book as well as many of the links to other sites. Almost everyone who was interviewed for this book was contacted by e-mail and responded to the authors' questions by e-mail. In addition, a substantial portion of the research for this book was done on the Internet. The authors are truly cybersurfers.

CYBERSURFERS
& Other
Online Types

CHAPTER ONE

A Look at the Internet

*Careers for Cybersurfers
and Other Online Types*

M ore than twenty-five million people worldwide use the Internet regularly. By 2001, this number may increase to as many as 250 million people. At first, Net users were primarily computer professionals, but this is changing rapidly. You'll find just about everybody online now, from businesspeople to students to housewives. There's a hermit in Egypt who is e-mailing the progress of an archaeological dig to American school children. There's a surfer in Australia going aboard the Net for surf reports. Queen Elizabeth II of England has her own 150-page Web site. The world is truly at the fingertips of all cybersurfers. They are using e-mail to communicate with people all around the world. They are accessing information from newspapers, magazines, and libraries and buying and selling products. These online aficionados of the Net are also playing games, listening to music, getting stock quotes, arbitrating disputes, finding medical advice, reading movie reviews, making virtual journeys to Mars, taking classes, ordering food, and finding jobs. These are just a few of the things that cybersurfers are doing today and a small fraction of what they will be doing on the Internet in the future.

What Is the Internet?

The Internet, also known as the Net, is the largest computer network in the world. It isn't a single network, but a network of networks interconnected by high-speed telephone wires. There are tens of thousands of these networks ranging in size from the big networks of corporate giants to small home networks with just a couple of PCs and everything in between. The number of these networks is growing each month. Every time you go aboard the Net, your own computer becomes an extension of that network. You can think of the Internet as being similar to a telephone system for it makes it possible to send information from place to place around the world.

A Brief History of the Internet

Historically, the Internet is very young. It grew out of the Department of Defense's desire in the 1960s to keep military sites in communication in the event of an enemy attack. What evolved was the Advanced Research Projects Administration Network (ARPANET), a network in which electronic traffic could be rerouted in case one of the network links was damaged or destroyed. It connected military sites, defense contractors, and colleges and universities. Soon other networks were developed, and operators began asking permission to connect their networks to ARPANET. The next major event in Internet history was the establishment in 1986 of a much faster network, NSFNET, by the National Science Foundation to connect supercomputer centers for research use. Then the foundation set up regional networks to link the users in each region, with the NSFNET connecting all the regional networks. Because NSFNET did not exclude people and institutions as ARPANET did, it became easy to become a part of this network simply by getting a connection to someone who was connected. Soon the network wasn't just being used for research but also for electronic mail, newsgroups, and file transfer; and large commercial networks were building their own networks, which they linked to NSFNET. The new network grew so rapidly and assumed so many functions of ARPANET that the older network was shut down in 1990.

By 1994, commercial firms had taken over the operation of the major network arteries, now collectively referred to as the Internet, and NSFNET was shut down a year later. In 1995, the Internet truly became a place for everyone to communicate, as so much appealing content appeared on the Internet, or Net. You can use your own computer to learn more about the history of the Internet by visiting ***http://www.info.isoc.org/guest/zakon/Internet/History/HIT.html***. In fact, throughout this book, you are going to be able to expand the information on the printed pages by going aboard the Net to visit the many sites mentioned in the text.

Main Features of the Internet

One of the main features of the Internet is the *World Wide Web* (www), or Web, as it is frequently called. Although Tim Berners-Lee thought of the www in 1989, it was not until 1993, with the development of the Mosaic Web Browser, that people could truly navigate the Web. Today, when people talk about "surfing the Net," they are usually talking about using the World Wide Web. What makes the Web the most appealing and fastest-growing part of the Internet are the home pages with their graphics and sound. You can jump from any place on the Web to any other place by clicking on a hypertext link (on-screen button, image, or line of text). The language that makes all of this possible is *HyperText Markup Language* (HTML). It also tells your Web browser how to display the contents of the page.

The most widely used Internet feature is *electronic mail* (e-mail). Any cybersurfer with access to the Internet can exchange messages with anyone else on an Internet-connected system.

The popularity of e-mail is astounding. It is rapidly replacing the interoffice memo at businesses and even replacing the telephone and mail as the way families and friends communicate with each other. Within twenty years, it may be as unusual not to have an e-mail address as it is not to have a phone today.

To discuss a topic with fellow cybersurfers, the Net feature that you want to use is the *newsgroup*. Almost any topic that you would ever wish to discuss now has a group talking about it on the Net. If you want to receive e-mail on a specific topic, you need only subscribe to another Net feature, the *mailing list*. Then information will be sent to you as well as to all the others on the list.

Internet Jobs—A Golden Opportunity for Cybersurfers

The Internet is now a career destination. In 1996, about 1.1 million Internet-related jobs were created in the United States, according to Harris Miller, president of the Information Technology Association of America. This should be excellent news for cybersurfers and other online types since a very real opportunity exists for them to find jobs associated with the Net. Because of the explosive growth of the Net, there is a tremendous shortage of skilled workers with degrees in computer science and engineering, and new positions have emerged such as Webmasters and graphic design artists and editors for the Web. Businesses are now looking for Internet-friendly employees who know how to access information on the Internet, put information on Web pages, and promote business on the Net. There is a demand for librarians with technical skills to organize the hundreds of thousands of pieces of information going onto the Net every year. In addition, opportunities exist for entrepreneurs to start companies that provide a service or sell a product on the Internet.

The list of Internet-related jobs is very long. In the next eight chapters, you will learn what some of these jobs are. *Caution*: the Internet is in its infancy and growing rapidly. You will need to surf the Net to keep abreast of all the new career opportunities that are constantly emerging. Be sure to make reading this book an interactive experience by visiting many of the sites that are given in the text. This will enhance what you are learning about careers for cybersurfers and other online types. Here is a brief overview of some of the jobs that you will read about in this book.

Jobs Providing Access to the Net

One of the fastest-growing areas in the Internet is providing access to the Net. Jobs are available at commercial online services such as America Online (AOL) and Microsoft Network (MSN) and at national, regional, and local Internet Service Providers (ISPs). If you work at AOL, you will be working with five thousand other employees. Should you choose to work at a small local service provider, there may only be one or two employees. Within every service provider, there are jobs for both technical and administrative personnel.

Jobs Outfitting Internetters with the Proper Hardware

If you want to be part of creating Internet hardware, you will typically work at one of the major equipment vendors; however, you could work at a small start-up company. Either way, you are more likely to be working in California than anywhere else. You could work as a hardware engineer actively involved in the design and development of hardware. Assemblers, inspectors, technicians, production staff, product managers, quality-control experts, sales and marketing people, education specialists, technical writers, and maintenance people also play key roles in providing the hardware needed for the Internet.

Jobs Developing Internet Software Tools

Even though many people are involved in developing software, the central figure is the programmer. This job requires extraordinary attention to detail. Creativity is also an asset. Because programmers often work as part of a team, they need to have solid oral and written communication skills. Professional programmers often have degrees in computer science or a related field. However, many have little or no formal instruction in programming.

Jobs Helping Companies Get on the Net

Just about every company has a presence on the Internet or is thinking about jumping aboard the Net. In order to do this, most companies need help from a varied group of people. Internet service providers design, host, and maintain Web sites. Cybermall operators provide electronic storefronts on the Net for companies selling products or services. Marketing and advertising experts work together to promote companies' products and services. Consultants offer financial, marketing, and technical advice.

Jobs Working as a Webmaster

Webmasters are in charge of the day-to-day operations of Web sites. Frequently, they work with a team consisting of marketing, technical, content, and public relations specialists. What responsibilities Webmasters have varies with where they work. Nevertheless, they always have the ultimate responsibility of making sure that Web sites project the presence that companies wish to have on the Net.

Jobs Providing a Unique Service on the Net

Help a person use the Internet to find a job, take a college course, play a game, check a bank balance, learn more about a sports hero, or plan a trip—these are just a few of the unique services available on the Internet, and more are constantly coming aboard. Be a technical whiz and help a service be delivered to cybersurfers. Or you can do such things as create, promote, market, or help customers use the service. You'll find jobs at such diverse places as banks, brokerage houses, online employment agencies, newspapers and magazines, and universities.

Jobs for Entrepreneurs: Selling Products Online

Sales on the Internet are not booming yet; however, as the number of people on the Internet increases, so will the opportunity to sell products online. You don't have to be a seasoned entrepreneur or spend a fortune to start a Net business. Many entrepreneurs are only in their twenties, and some have spent $2,500 or less to establish a business. What you do need to succeed is knowledge, dedication, and hard work.

More Jobs for Cybersurfers

Every day cybersurfers are going aboard the Internet and finding more jobs associated with the Net because it is growing so explosively. You can teach anything from graduate-level classes to cooking or novel writing. You can search on the Net for information for other people or companies. You can visit Web sites all day and write site reviews. There are jobs for you in the government, libraries, or in your own home connected to the Net.

Jobs in the Future

No one can predict the future with 100 percent accuracy. People were not able to guess at all the new jobs that would appear after the invention of the automobile, telephone, or television. The scenario will be the same for Internet jobs.

Finding an Internet Job

Cybersurfers seeking a job associated with the Internet—or any other job—can use the Internet to ease their search. The career resources of the Net are stupendous. You will find huge databases of job listings and be able to search for a job anytime, twenty-four hours a day, seven days a week. You can post your resume in databases and newsgroups where prospective employers will see it. You'll be able to find out about jobs whether they are in Topeka, Kansas, or in Tokyo. You can network with other cybersurfers to find out about companies and possible job openings. You can even chat with career counselors and practice your interview skills online. Also, you can go to a company's Web site to learn more about it and to see what job opportunities may be available.

One of the very best resources on the Internet for learning about employment opportunities and job resources is *The Riley Guide* at **http://www.jobtrak.com/jobguide**. It will tell you how to incorporate the Internet in your job search, find Net career planning services, prepare your resume for the Net, and find the best research sources for your job search. An excellent print resource is *The Guide to Internet Job Searching* by Margaret Riley, Frances Roehm, and Steve Oserman.

Applying for Jobs Advertised on the Internet

Many employers are now asking job applicants to apply by e-mail. If you are going to apply for a job online, you will need an online resume. This is a plain document text. It is not the mail version of your resume, but one that is specially done so it will look good after it has been e-mailed. In order to find out how to write an online resume, look at online resources like these: Joyce Lain Kennedy, "How to Write an Electronic Resume," **http://www.occ.com/occ/JLK/HowToEResume.html**, and Fred Nagel, "Resume Tips from Acorn Career Counseling and Resume Writing," *http://1.mhv.net/~acorn/Acorn.html*. Or you could read one of the following books: *Electronic Resume Revolution* by Joyce Lain Kennedy and Thomas J. Morrow and *Using the Internet in Your Job Search* by Fred E. Jandt and Mary B. Nemmich. After you have completed your online resume, always be sure to e-mail it to yourself or a friend to check how it looks.

How Much Can You Expect to Earn?

The easiest way to find salary information on jobs associated with the Internet is to use the Net. Go to JobSmart's site, *http://jobsmart.org*, where you will find a quick guide to salary surveys and links to more than 120 salary surveys. Follow Job-Smart's advice in evaluating the information in terms of how current it is, its geographic coverage, and your own situation. If you can't find the information you need at this site, look at Margaret Riley's December 5, 1996, article in *National Business Employment Weekly* at *http://www.NBEW.com* for more solid suggestions about places to look such as trade and professional associations and journals.

Qualifications for Internet Jobs

Organizations will not hire you just because you enjoy surfing the Net; however, your ability to move skillfully around the Internet is a tremendous plus for so many jobs. Internet companies as well as businesses that are on the Net respect college degrees. A degree in computer science or computer engineering is an immediate ticket to a job in today's job market. If you will not be working in a position developing Net hardware or software, a technical major is not necessary. However, computer literacy is a requirement for almost every job, and this includes knowing how to use e-mail and to navigate the Internet. Audrey Iwata, a personnel manager and college recruiter for Pacific Bell, believes that having a high level of expertise about the Internet and all of its applications only increases an applicant's marketability—online or off.

CHAPTER TWO

Providing Access to the Internet

P roviding access to the Internet is one of the fastest-growing areas in the Internet business world. Both companies and individuals are clamoring for connection to the Net. There is also intense competition among access providers to sign up new customers. The whole scene is changing so rapidly that it is difficult to predict today who will be the major players of tomorrow. Overall, there is a tremendous need for qualified people who understand the new medium with which they are dealing. From technicians to software engineers, from service representatives to marketing professionals, the demand for people is high at companies providing access to the Internet.

An Overview of Access Providers

When you first think of a job associated with offering Internet access, you may immediately think of working at an online service provider such as America Online or Microsoft Network. These companies, however, are decidedly not the only ones involved in providing Net access. To know where all the jobs are in this area, you need to understand how the Internet is built.

Traffic speeds across the Internet on *backbones*, or very high-capacity lines. Network Access Points (NAPs) offer interconnections to national and regional backbone operators. The backbone operators in turn offer connections to the online service providers, Internet service providers, and large businesses. Consumers and smaller businesses generally connect to a service provider. The following diagram shows how traffic flows on the Internet.

You can find jobs with NAPs, backbone operators, online service providers, Internet service providers, and large businesses.

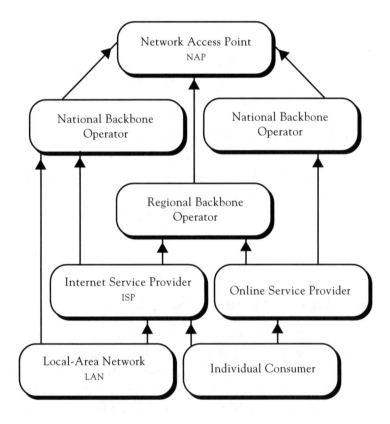

Figure 2.1
Internet Traffic Pattern

Network Access Points

The NAPs provide the basis for interconnectivity between the backbone operators. They are the physical points where the backbones connect and exchange information. There are three official NAPs as well as several other access points that perform the same function. The following Web sites offer information on the NAPs, and most include descriptions of available jobs:

- Chicago Network Access Point, Ameritech Advanced Data Services and Bellcorp
  http://www.ameritech.com/products/data/nap/

- New York Network Access Point, SprintLink
  www.sprintlink.net

- San Francisco Network Access Point, Pacific Bell
  www.pacbell.com/Products/NAP/

- Metropolitan Area Ethernets (MAE)
  http://ext2.mfsdatanet.com/MAE/

- CIX Commercial Internet Exchange
  http://www.cix.org

- Federal Internet Exchange (FIX)
  http://www.arc.nasa.gov

National and Regional Backbone Operators

Companies that function as backbone operators have high-speed TCP/IP (Transfer Control Protocol/Internet Protocol) routers connected by data transmission lines leased from long-distance exchange carriers. They usually connect several major cities with high-speed T3 leased lines and extend those connections to surrounding areas with the slower T1 lines. This

creates a network that is often made up of several hundred cities and towns.

The backbones offer direct connections to businesses and Internet service providers through machines called gateways, or IP routers, which remain continuously online. These are expensive connections requiring a heavy initial outlay for equipment and software as well as ongoing costs for leasing dedicated telephone lines and providing continuing support. In addition to offering dedicated connections, the backbones may also contain divisions that act as service providers.

At this time the Internet is in a period of rapid expansion. All backbone providers are extending their services, adding new lines and new customers at an unbelievable rate.

Major Backbone Operators

Visit the Web sites of the major backbone operators to learn more about the services they provide. Many will also tell about employment opportunities.

AGIS	*http://www.agis.net*
ANS	*http://www.ans.net*
AT&T WorldNet	*http://www.att.com/worldnet*
BBN Planet	*http://www.bbn.com*
MCI	*http://infopage.mci.net/*
Sprint	*http://www.sprint.com*
PSI	*http://wwwpipeline.com*
UUNet/AlterNet	*http://www.uunet.com*

A National Backbone Operator

BBN Planet/AT&T WorldNet has been involved with the Internet since its earliest beginnings. BBN Planet's parent company was the design firm that essentially built ARPANET, the forerunner to today's Internet. Headquartered in Cambridge, Massachusetts, BBN Planet maintains a T3 backbone connecting thirteen cities, with additional cities connected by T1 lines.

BBN's customer base is made up of businesses, governmental customers, and universities. AT&T WorldNet has an agreement with BBN Planet to resell access as a business and consumer dial-up service. AT&T announced its service in February of 1996 and by May had 150,000 customers.

BBN Planet has a primary network operations center staffed twenty-four hours a day as well as two operations support centers. They employ over five hundred people, including field service staff, consulting service engineers, and applications design personnel.

Online Service Providers

Online service providers are the large commercial services such as America Online, CompuServe, Microsoft Network, and Prodigy. You are probably familiar with these names. These services are traditionally the first access points for the beginning online explorer. They offer a great deal of general-interest information and family-oriented content, provide e-mail and World Wide Web access, and offer a browser to navigate the Net. Ease of installation is a plus for beginners.

The major online providers are to some degree distinguished by the types of services they offer. Prodigy features graphics-based multiplayer games and general news; CompuServe is known for its technical support and large file download areas;

and America Online offers access to national magazines and search databases. On the negative side, the services offer only an indirect connection; their computers are interposed between the customer and the Internet, exerting a controlling influence on the information exchange.

The growth of online service providers has mirrored the growth of the Internet. Competition to acquire customers is intense. In particular, AOL would like to build television-size audiences as a method to ensure profitability, but at the time we are writing, AOL's rapid growth has eroded its level of service and has consequently affected customer satisfaction. AOL is desperately striving to add both equipment and customer-support personnel to handle the explosive growth.

Further information about the major online service providers and employment opportunities at these companies is available at the following Web sites:

America Online	*http://www-db.aol.com/corp*
CompuServe	*http://www/compuserve.com*
Prodigy	*http://www.prodigy.com*
Microsoft	*http://www.msn.com*

An Online Service Provider

America Online serves over eight million customers throughout the United States and overseas. AOL is headquartered in Dulles, Virginia, and has three main divisions. The AOL Networks division aggressively develops new sources of revenue through interactive marketing programs, advertising, and online transactions. It offers its subscribers e-mail, Internet access, news, sports, weather, financial information and transactions, and electronic shopping. A second division, ANS Access, operates the world's largest data communications network,

with more than 160,000 modems connecting 472 cities in the United States and an additional 152 cities internationally. It also operates AOL GlobalNet, offering access in an additional 230 cities in eighty-three countries. The third division is AOL Studios, which will develop interactive programming.

America Online currently has more than five thousand employees. You may find job openings in the following fields:

Account Management	Accounting
Administration	Business Development
Consulting	Content Producers
Content Programming	Design
Editing/Writing	Engineering
Finance	Information Technology
Information Technology Management	Legal
Marketing	Member Services
Network Operations	Production Management
Product Marketing Management	Programming Management
Software Development	Software Testing
Systems Administration	Technology
Training and Education	

If you visit the AOL Web site, you will be able to investigate career opportunities such as the following jobs. Note the diversity of jobs, and be sure to notice the qualifications needed for positions that interest you.

Junior Programmer in the Technology Department

Education Requirement: Bachelor's degree

Professional Experience: All experience levels

Job Description: Entry-level programmer trained in C and UNIX. Maintain legacy ordering systems written in PL1 on Stratus. Assist in porting such systems to C and UNIX. Fluent in C and UNIX; good problem-solving skills.

Programmer/Analyst in the Technology Department

Education Requirement: High School

Professional Experience: four to six years

Job Description: Responsible for analysis, design, and implementation of Electronic Commerce systems written in C on a UNIX platform. Responsible for full development life cycle of interactive electronic commerce systems. Will gather requirements, design, code, and test such systems. Five or more years of experience with C++ on UNIX platform; realtime, user-interface applications; relational DB (sybase a plus).

Shift Supervisor in the Technology Department

Education Requirement: High School

Professional Experience: four to six years

Job Description: Manage day-to-day activities of Security Response Center staff and be first escalation point for complex issues. Handle special customer service requests. Manage work and vacations scheduling for SRC staff. Audit computer rights and access for all AOL employees. AOL, Stratus, UNIX, spreadsheet, organizational skills, good customer service focus, strong general technical skills.

Some missionaries are ordained priests or ministers. However, additional technical skills or areas of expertise are looked upon with favor.

Upon completion of formal schooling, most missionaries spend time in an apprenticed position working with veteran missionaries. During this time, they gain a firsthand knowledge and understanding of the culture and language of their host countries.

Some colleges allow students to serve as interns—an experience that allows them to find out what it is like, more or less, to be a missionary. DePauw University, for example, offers students the opportunity to spend one month as missionaries. During past years, students have assisted Guatemalans caught in earthquakes, helped to bring electricity to a small Peruvian village, and were involved in many other positive deeds in diverse areas of the world.

Personal characteristics that are desirable for those wishing to pursue missionary work include the ability to be independent, the desire to make a difference in the world by helping people, the ability to adapt to surroundings no matter how difficult they are, the facility to learn a new language quickly, the knack of being a team player, and the skill to assess situations quickly and act upon them as necessary. Other positive attributes include patience, fortitude, and empathy. Since missionaries are often on call twenty-four hours a day, it is important to be physically and mentally strong. Last, but certainly not least, a positive, sunny disposition and sense of humor are great assets.

Though advancement is usually not a priority, it is possible to work up to serving on a mission board or heading a large mission and supervising a number of other missionaries.

Sometimes the pattern of life that has been set for missionaries doesn't end when they return home or complete their initial term of service. Individuals often continue their support of such as MCI and Sprint; corporations such as IBM; and telephone companies such as U.S. West and Pacific Bell.

The Telephone Companies

Five of the "Baby Bells" have announced plans to jointly market Internet access to seventy-two million customers in twenty-six states in conjunction with Netscape's popular Web browser. The Bells say that they can use their network building ability to provide a service as reliable as today's basic phone service. Netscape's ISP Select program will allow users to automatically create a new telephone company account directly from their computer. Customers' Internet billing will be added to their phone bills. The Bells hope to offer each customer a local calling number that will allow Internet access anywhere in the United States without long-distance charges.

Regional and Local
Internet Service Providers

The majority of ISPs are local and regional companies that generally operate in just a few area codes and increasingly offer a high level of customer service and technical support. Their rapid growth reflects the consumer demand for both faster access to the Net and increased customer service. They are a direct beneficiary of the growth problems being encountered by the online services.

A Regional Internet Service Provider

Jim Deibele started Teleport in 1987 with one PC in a spare bedroom. Today, Teleport is the largest Internet provider in the Northwest, serving Oregon and Southwest Washington, with four separate T1 lines connecting twenty thousand subscribers.

Teleport employs about forty people in a community-oriented business. It offers support and special discounts to teachers, librarians, and nonprofit organizations.

In addition to providing standard consumer access accounts, Teleport also offers a virtual server account. A virtual server allows you to run your Web site on an ISP's server as if your Web site had its own dedicated Internet connection. Your Web address would look like: ***http://www.yourname.com***. A virtual server account is able to give the Web site operator detailed statistics on which of his Web pages are being accessed and how often they are accessed; this information can be of great help to a business when making marketing decisions.

A Success Story—Jim Deibele and Teleport

In 1987, Jim owned a bookstore specializing in technical books. Many of his customers would ask him to e-mail them when their special orders arrived. Jim saw a need for e-mail and began providing this service from a 386 computer with eight megabytes of RAM (random-access memory) and five hundred megabytes of disk space. In 1989, he upgraded his equipment, added four modems, and began charging $5.00 a month—twice the rates of the competition, but Jim advertised that his connections were always available. In 1992, Jim offered his first Internet connection, using a 14.4-speed modem.

Jim's make-or-break year was 1993. His bookstore had folded, and a national ISP had announced its intention to offer Internet access in Portland. Jim worked as a temp to make money to buy better modems for his business. If 1993 was his toughest year, 1994 was his best. Teleport hired its first employee in August, the same day the firm incorporated; three more were hired later that same year; and in October, Jim was finally able to take a salary for himself. Now he is no longer doing everything from being the receptionist to handling the billing but is hiring people who specialize in certain areas.

The Teleport Job Profile

You can learn more about the jobs at a regional Internet service provider by the studying the organization of Teleport as well as the descriptions of several of the positions.

- President and Founder

- Senior Vice President, Marketing and Communications

- Director of Operations

- System Administration: Manager, three operators

- Technical Support: Manager, Assistant Manager, Senior Technician, Internal Support Technician, thirteen staff members

- Office Staff: Manager, two Receptionists, one staff member

- Billing Staff: Supervisor, two other positions

- Creative Services: Webmaster, Art Director, Designer, Researcher, CGI Programmer

- Outreach: one staff member

- Nonprofits Coordinator: one staff member

- Teleport Sales: one staff member

Technical Support

Pay ranges from $8.00 to $10.00 per hour, perhaps somewhat higher for someone who is really qualified. Most ISPs have a layered system of two or three levels with the most senior staff acting as resource specialists for junior staff. Teleport prefers to hire people with good customer service skills, feeling that it is always possible train for the technical skills. Currently, Teleport wishes to increase support personnel to twenty-four and is having difficulty hiring.

Creative Services

Pay begins at $12.00 per hour. Creative Services' personnel generally work for all the customers. Salaries for these positions are not as high as they would be at a marketing or public relations firm.

System Administration

Pay starts at $30.00 for system administration positions. Teleport reports a problem finding qualified people in this area.

Overview of Jobs

Jeff Shannon, in charge of outreach at Teleport, reports a trend among the rapidly growing ISPs to offer "twenty-four-by-seven" or twenty-four-hour-a-day, seven-day-a-week *technical support*. This is the most labor-intensive position in most ISPs. Jeff calls the technical support staff "real bridge people" because of the connection they provide between the ISP and the consumer. He feels this is a transferable skill in that a good "Tech" can go anywhere and find a job. Jeff also sees continued demand for *systems operators* who can understand and manipulate the backbone and for *creative services* personnel who are versed in the Web authoring languages such as CGI, HTML, and PERL.

A Local Internet Service Provider

Cruzio is one of the oldest and largest network providers in Santa Cruz County, California. It differs from the larger online services in that it offers a community-based, community-oriented connection to the Internet. Cruzio's home page offers links to sixteen areas of community information ranging from the arts to weather, tides, and surf. It offers information on "Local Hot Spots" and two "Live (more or less) Cameras." Cruzio also has a Web page devoted to "Surfn' Santa Cruz—

the one-stop Web page for all the information you need to plan and enjoy surfing in this beach resort town."

Owners Peggy Dolgenos and her husband began their careers as software engineers working for a large software company. They had used the Internet and e-mail since the 1980s and felt that these would be useful tools to offer schools and seniors as a community service. They opened Cruzio in 1989, and it took off.

Peggy says that owning a small business is a twenty-four-hour-a-day, seven-day-a-week job. She compares an ISP to a public utility in that service must always be maintained. She is on a pager day and night, as the owner is the end of the line of responsibility and must always be ready to respond to problems—at 5:00 A.M. if necessary. Looking toward the future, she feels that there will always be a niche for the smaller ISP. The Internet is not like TV because with the Net there is actually interaction. People write letters as well as read them. The community ISP is able to meet this need for a higher level of service.

The Future of Local and Regional ISPs

Starting a new Internet service provider business is much more difficult today than when Teleport or Cruzio were started. People's expectations have changed dramatically over the past few years, and it now takes a substantial amount of money to buy the equipment to provide the necessary level of service.

Jim Deibele believes that there will eventually be between six hundred and six thousand of these local and regional ISPs. The consumer doesn't care who provides the service, just that it is efficient. According to Jim, the smaller-scale ISPs are quicker to realize that what worked yesterday is not going to work tomorrow, whether it is the phone system or the help-desk software. Their engineers are also better able to fine-tune specific locations.

Other Points of Access

Should you decide that you want to help people access the Internet, even more choices await you. An ever-increasing number of options are appearing for accessing the Net.

Area Networks: LAN and WAN

LANs (Local Area Networks) are limited networks, often owned by businesses and universities, that link computers together with other equipment within a small geographic area. WANs (Wide Area Networks) connect individual groups with an infrastructure often rented from an Internet service provider. LANs and WANs increasingly are linked to the Internet, although the link may be filtered. This development has created a group of people well versed in Internet skills and interested in establishing Internet links at home.

vBNS—The Scientists Network

A very high speed Backbone Network System (vBNS) has just been opened for scientific use. Built and maintained by MCI Telecommunications, it is more than twenty-one thousand times faster than the average modem. It is so fast that an entire digital-quality two-hour movie could be downloaded in a matter of seconds. Administrators at the National Science Foundation decide which researchers and projects can have access to the new network. It is expected that it will be five to ten years before the Internet is capable of running at this speed.

Schools and Libraries

There is increasing determination across the entire nation to see that our schools are connected to the Net. There have been calls for setting aside a portion of the radio frequency spectrum for unlicensed wireless digital communications for schools, libraries, and health care facilities. This would allow LANs to be established without the necessity of hardwiring buildings. The LANs would in turn connect to the Net. If this new technology can support the higher speed demands of the ever-evolving Internet, then its greatly reduced cost should lead to rapid and widespread adoption and create a demand for both equipment and instructors.

Office Services

Connections to the Internet may be made at various office service companies such as Kinko's Copies. Currently, Kinko's only offers connections to previously established personal accounts held with the online services, but it plans to expand its Internet access in the near future.

Internet Telephony

Several new services allow people to make phone calls over the Internet rather than over expensive long-distance lines. Microsoft, Intel, and Netscape are currently working on computer-to-computer voice communications. Other new products allow people to bypass the computer and speak through regular phones over the Internet. Finally, the telephone companies can offer Internet calling as a service, charging an access fee, as they already have an Internet infrastructure in place. Any of these developments would open up new employment opportunities.

Future Job Trends—A Note of Caution

With all the enthusiasm over the growth of the Internet, it is important to realize that some of the very developments contributing to the growth of the Net are also causing a decline in certain jobs. Sophisticated software programs have lessened the

ISPs' need for large numbers of software engineers. Additionally, the mergers and consolidations of cable and telephone companies, in conjunction with the development of increasingly sophisticated equipment, may lead to an actual decrease in the number of installers and repairers employed by the telephone companies.

For further information on Internet service providers, look for copies of the following magazines or check their Web sites:

Boardwatch	***http://www.boardwatch.com***
NetGuide	***http://www.netguidemag.com***
Internet World	***http://www.iw.com***

CHAPTER THREE

Outfitting Companies and Individuals with the Proper Hardware

Y ou might consider that the Internet, in its simplest form, is composed of three basic parts:

1. The lines, which are most often supplied by the telephone company.

2. The hubs, routers, and switches that connect those lines.

3. The individual computer and its associated equipment.

All of these parts of the system are called *hardware*, while all the programs that make the equipment work are called *software*. Those who are actively involved in the design and development of hardware are usually called *hardware engineers*. Assemblers, inspectors, technicians, production staff, product managers, quality control experts, sales and marketing people, education specialists, technical writers, and maintenance people also play key roles in bringing Internet hardware to individuals and companies.

If you want to be part of creating Net hardware, you will typically work at one of the major equipment vendors such as Cisco Systems or Bay Networks or at a line provider such as Pacific Bell or Ameritech. Today's network is composed of equipment that is designed to work together regardless of the manufacturer, using the common standard TCP/IP, or Transfer Control Protocol/Internet Protocol. This is called "open architecture" and is partly responsible for the proliferation of manufacturers as well as the rapid development of new technologies.

When each part of a system works with everyone else's part, then a new component of a system can be developed and integrated without having to rebuild the entire system. Small startup firms are able to get their products to a market that is no longer the exclusive province of the major firms. You may find a job within a large, well-established company or at a newly established company; you are more likely to work in California than anywhere else, as 43.5 percent of the computer companies are located in California and 40 percent of all Internet traffic is generated there.

The Hubs, Routers, and Switches

Hubs, routers, and network switches are the devices responsible for moving the Internet traffic to its destination. AOL and other ISPs have had to add routers and other network equipment every eighteen months to service their rapid expansion. The industry involved in building these tools is expected to grow 50 percent in the next year alone. Visit the Web sites of the top four companies, which together control 85 percent of the industry's revenues and 90 percent of the profits for company and employment information:

Cisco Systems	*http://www.cisco.com*
Bay Networks	*http://www.baynetworks.com*
3Com	*http://www.3com.com*
Cabletron	*http://www.cabletron.com*

How They Work

Switches, routers, and hubs all do the same thing, to some degree, in that they direct the traffic on the Internet. When you think of *switches*, think of the telephone companies (Telcos) and local area networks. A *router* defines a fork in the road based on established rules. Routers sense traffic on a network and route that traffic over a wide area connection. Additionally, routers talk to each other, continuously sending messages about their current load. *Hubs* are where the wires come together in a central location.

The cloud in the diagram is a standard depiction of the Internet.

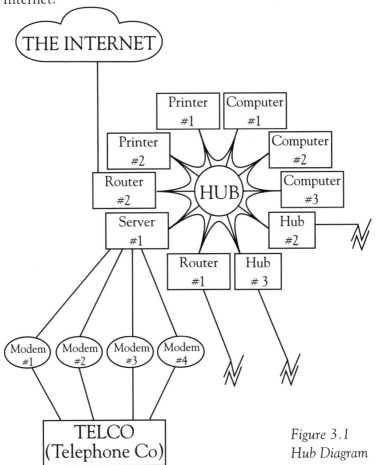

Figure 3.1
Hub Diagram

A *packet* is an amount of data, of a fixed size, encapsulated with addressing and routing information. It is convenient to visualize it as a gel capsule such as one that might contain aspirin or vitamins.

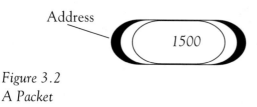

Figure 3.2
A Packet

All files are broken up into packets. The number of packets depends on the size of the file.

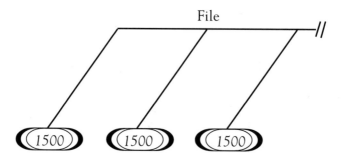

Figure 3.3
File/Packet Diagram

To transmit a file from California to the East Coast, you throw all the packets out into the cloud (the Internet), the switches gobble them up, and the routers send them on their way. Some packets may go through Houston and some through Minneapolis, but they are all reassembled at their destination. If a packet gets lost on the way, the destination point notifies the sender and a replacement packet is transmitted. All of this occurs in a short period of time and is invisible to the user.

A Company Profile: Cisco Systems

Cisco Systems was founded in 1984 by computer scientists from Stanford University who believed that an easier way to connect computer systems was needed. This multinational corporation with $4 billion in annual revenue and 9,700 employees has its headquarters in San Jose, California.

Cisco makes about 80 percent of the routers used to decipher and direct traffic on the Internet. Cisco also makes the LAN and ATM switches that will experience a huge surge in demand as Internet data traffic explodes. Other Cisco products include dial-up access servers and network management software, which should continue to experience strong demand as businesses continue to use Internet solutions to establish office Intranets, or private internal network resources.

Cisco recently had one thousand job openings listed and was hiring at the rate of twelve persons a day. For current information on available jobs, check Cisco's Web site at ***http:// www.cisco.com/jobs/***.

Making the Connection

Everyone wants a faster connection, and to a major extent this is determined by the type of line you use. Most consumers connect to an ISP using POTS (plain old telephone service) through a 14.4 kilobytes per second (kbps) or 28.8 kbps modem. A faster connection for the home or small business user is an ISDN (Integrated Services Digital Network) line, already available in some areas, which operates at 64 kbps or 128 kbps. Both POTS and ISDN are on-demand lines, which means you are not connected to the Net until you sign on. Many companies use lines that are switched or dedicated and operate at 56 kbps. A switched line has dial-up service (you only pay for what you use), while a dedicated line is always connected to the Internet and is used by companies needing full-time access. A T1 line is the backbone of the telephone infrastructure. When it is directly connected to a company, it offers the highest speed Internet connection available. A T3 line carries twenty-eight times the capacity of a T1 line and is most often used by the nation's backbone providers.

ISDN (Integrated Services Digital Network)

The cost of direct T1 connections to the Internet puts them beyond the reach of most individuals. ISDN lines are a partial solution. They upgrade today's standard analog telephone network to a digital system. With the exception of the part running from the local exchange to your office or home, the world's telephone network is already digital. ISDN upgrades that final link of the system. With ISDN, you can be online and talk on the phone over the same line at the same time. ISDN operates at speeds up to 128 kbps, which is at least five times faster than today's analog modems. It is especially helpful in speeding up the transfer of rich media, such graphics and audio and visual applications. It is available in most urban and suburban areas.

Coming in the future is ADSL, which stands for Asymmetric Digital Subscriber Line. It is asymmetric in that you will be able to receive a lot a data but you will be limited in the amount you can send back. Even faster lines are being planned by the telephone companies, but they may be challenged by cable TV and wireless methods, including cellular, microwave, and satellite.

For further information on high-speed lines, check the following Web sites:

ISDN	*http://www.4PBISDN*
ADSL	*http://www.telechoice.com/ xdsinewz/BackMat.html*

Working with ISDN

William Moore describes himself as a software guy gone bad. With a degree in computer science from the University of California at San Diego, he now works for a major telephone company as a second-level manager in data products. He works with ISDN in market and channel development brand management. His firm put ISDN at retail in 1995 and in August of that year William approached Microsoft about ISDN. Windows 95 now has support programs for ISDN, and you can order an ISDN line on the Microsoft Web site.

William is the Webmaster for his company's ISDN Web site. Although he oversees the program, he contracts with outside firms to provide employees to work on specific areas of his Web site, such as the back-end database. William says the value of the Web is "just smoking," particularly for advertising and electronic commerce. A good Web site can often make things easier for customers to find the information they want, thus generating higher customer satisfaction. William tries to work with the attitude: "What can I do today to make a significant impact?"

Working with Other Types of Hardware

Hardware is continuously being created and modified as developments in technology offer new choices. These are exciting times for those of you who want jobs that will change the face of the Internet as we know it. Remember, the Internet is just in its infancy. Today's Internet is more like Henry Ford's Model T than the sleek, fast car that you drive. Imagine being a part of developing some of the new Net hardware that we will be seeing in the next ten years.

Modems are faster already with 33.6 kbps becoming common and a 56 kbps modem on the horizon. *ISDN modems* and *cable modems* are now being used due to the increasing availability of new types of access. There are *satellite dishes* that provide downstream Web access at about 400 kbps. Uploads and data requests are still via analog modem, but the downloads are by satellite.

The *Web on TV* has arrived via an Internet appliance that is simple to use and is half the size of a VCR. In the works is a stripped-down *dedicated computer* that will allow you to surf the Web and get e-mail while storing your files on your ISP's computer. *Cable-free Internet access* for your notebook computer is now available due to advances in infrared technology. There is also a *receiver* that plugs into your computer and, using the same wireless technology employed by pagers, provides continuous Internet news and e-mail alerts without a dedicated connection.

How about a cordless *Internet controller*, allowing you to sit back in comfort when surfing the Web? Good news for couch potatoes. *Sound cards* and *video cards* are becoming increasingly sophisticated to take advantage of the multimedia offered on the Web. The top *monitors* are able to display brighter colors and better contrast and handle graphics easily. MMX (multimedia extensions) technology allows PCs to deliver images quicker and in more TV-like fashion. A new *T1 chip* will allow users to download files 120 times faster than they can today. An *Internet phone* lets you use your computer as a telephone. *Computer Telephony Integration* (CTI) is the convergence of computer and telephone technology. Someday, through multicasting, your telephone, your TV, your computer, and your radio will all be part of the same system for which you will pay a single flat fee.

The Internet is on a continuous cycle where each advance in programs and services stimulates a demand for increased speed, and each advance in speed opens up a new area of possible services. The market for people to design and build Internet hardware will be strong for the foreseeable future, although just which line or piece of hardware will be the standard in the future is still to be determined.

Connecting It All

Don Jensen keeps 110 people at Granite Construction Company connected to the Internet. He runs an Intranet, a private internal resource, which connects to a national ISP offering dedicated connections of 56 kbps which are each one-twenty-fourth of a T1 connection. The company's main hub is located in Watsonville, California, and the others are in Dallas, Atlanta, and Tampa.

Each of the 110 company employees has his or her own Internet address. While an ISP with ten subscribers per modem is generally considered to offer good service, Don has arranged for the company to have almost a one-to-one ratio, as many of the employees are online all day long. Granite Construction Company also has an 800 number so that workers who are traveling can easily plug in their laptops from a hotel room.

Don is responsible for installing and maintaining all the equipment as well as for training the personnel in the use of the Internet. By connecting people to the home office using the Internet, Don has saved the company a minimum of $21,000 per month in long-distance telephone bills. His work hours are long when he is out of the main office. On the road, Don frequently works at night because the company offices are so busy during the day. The most interesting part of his job, Don finds, is giving a system to a new user who has only heard about the Internet and never used it. The Net neophyte usually can't believe the speed of communication and data links available on the Internet.

Don points out that if you work with hardware, you must keep up with the technology or you'll find your job skills obsolete. The emergence of the Internet is like a moving river—you need to swim with it and realize that it is going to be different every year. For this reason, it is very important for workers in this area to be the type of employee who welcomes change. In Don's field, equipment will become easier to run; however, there will always be a need for someone to take the computer, put it on someone's desk, and teach him or her how to run it.

Developing Your Own Career in Hardware

If you are seriously thinking about a career in the Internet industry, you must keep track of current trends in order to make solid career decisions. Competition is so fierce and innovation so rapid in the Internet industry that giant firms can stumble and newcomers can rapidly disappear. Furthermore, much of your value to your employer will depend on your knowledge of the latest technologies in the hardware field. You will need to continue your education throughout your career.

One possible job avenue to consider is working abroad. A great number of jobs are going to open up in other countries. The pioneer spirit has greatly influenced the development of the Internet in the United States. Companies have been willing to invest a lot of money simply on faith, a model that works well in this country. Businesses in many foreign countries have felt the need to quantify the value of every undertaking and have been slower to hop aboard the Net bandwagon. Eventually, they will need help in adopting the new technologies or risk being left behind.

Here is a close look at several jobs in the hardware industry. Perhaps one of them will appeal to you.

Electronic Engineers

Electronic engineers design, develop, test, and supervise the manufacture of electronic equipment. They also write performance requirements and develop maintenance schedules. A bachelor's degree is usually required for these positions, with many job applicants having a master's degree. Pay starts at $35,000 per year, with the median pay for midlevel engineers at about $54,400. Engineers at senior managerial levels receive a median salary of about $90,000. With the rapid expansion of the Internet, college graduates with knowledge of the latest technologies will continue to be in demand.

Systems Analysts

LANs (Local Area Networks) and WANs (Wide Area Networks) are frequently designed by systems analysts who use their knowledge and skills in a problem-solving capacity. They may design entirely new systems, combining hardware and software to allow free exchange of data. A growing number of systems analysts are employed on a temporary or contract basis or as consultants. A bachelor's degree in a computer-related field is almost always required. Median annual earnings of computer systems analysts are about $44,000. There is a continued demand by businesses for networking systems, which should ensure job opportunities for applicants whose skills are current.

Electronic Engineering Technicians

Electronic engineering technicians use their knowledge of electronic circuits to help design, develop, and manufacture electronic equipment. Many technicians assist engineers and scientists, especially in research and development. Prospective engineering technicians should take as many high school science and math courses as possible. Advanced training is required by most employers and is available at technical institutes, junior and community colleges, and extension divisions of four-year colleges and universities. Many employers emphasize the need for good communication skills and the ability to work with others as technicians often work as part of a team. At the beginning levels, salaries average between $14,560 and $19,500 a year. Those in senior or supervisory positions earn about $51,060. While technicians will remain in demand, the growing availability and use of advanced technologies is expected to curtail employment growth in this field.

Equipment Operators

As more and more establishments realize the need to connect all their computers in LANs (Local Area Networks) in order to enhance productivity, there will be an increasing demand for full-time operators. Sophisticated computer programs now enable the computer to perform many routine tasks formerly done by computer operators, whose attention now will be directed toward troubleshooting, desk help, system security, network problems, and maintenance of large databases. Previous work experience and some computer-related training, perhaps through a junior college, are job requirements in many large establishments. Full-time computer operators have median earnings of $21,300 a year, with the lowest 10 percent earning less than $12,800 and the top 10 percent earning more than $39,500.

Electronic Equipment Repairers

Electronic equipment repairers are also called service technicians or field service representatives. They install, maintain, and repair electronic equipment. As the number of computers in service increases, so will the demand for people to repair them. Median annual earnings of full-time electronic equipment repairers are $29,600.

CHAPTER FOUR

Developing Software

All the programs that make Internet and computer equipment work are called software. You are using software when you e-mail a friend, access a Web site, or download a file. Visit any store selling software and you will see the vast number of programs that have been created for business, pleasure, and education. Many individuals are involved in developing software, often delivering upgrades to the end user as an Internet download. There are careers in software for developers, salespeople, marketing experts, advertisers, teachers, trainers, writers, managers, and researchers. However, the central figure in the development of software remains the programmer.

In the past, systems analysts designed software programs to meet specific system needs, and programmers had the task of writing the programs to fill those needs. Today, these responsibilities and job titles are blurring; many individuals perform both tasks, especially in smaller firms. They write the programs (lists of instructions) that make computers act in a certain way, test the programs, debug the programs (correct errors), maintain and update the programs, and possibly even write the documentation (instructions on how to use a program or computer system effectively).

Being a programmer requires an ability to pay extraordinary attention to detail. Programmers must be able to think logically and concentrate on a task for long periods at a time. Creativity is also an asset for programmers who must find unusual solutions to resolve difficult problems. Both oral and written communication skills are important as programmers often work as part of a team. Professional programmers often have a bachelor's or master's degree in computer science or a related field such as electrical engineering. However, many excellent programmers have little or no formal instruction in programming. As in every career field related to the rapidly evolving Internet, it is of paramount importance that the programmer remains up-to-date on the latest developments in this field.

Internet Software Developments

Software developments are in large part responsible for the directions in which the Internet has grown. The Internet is made up of many different kinds of computers, from PCs to mainframes. TCP/IP (Transfer Control Protocol/Internet Protocol) is a system of protocols used by all computers that allows them to talk to each other. A protocol is a set of instructions used by computers to describe how information will be shared between them. Without a universal system like TCP/IP, computers could not communicate with each other and there would be no Internet. Many Net software programs are based on TCP/IP, such as FTP (File Transfer Protocol), Telnet, and World Wide Web browsers.

E-mail Needs Software Programs

E-mail was one of the first services developed for the Internet. Originally designed to exchange information, it has become a popular method for personal communication. It is also being increasingly used by business to allow clients to report problems and request information about services and products. One of the most widely used e-mail programs is Eudora, originally written for the Macintosh and now ported to Windows. More information about Eudora may be found at: ***http:// www.qualcomm.com/quest.***

HTML Is the Web Page Language

HTML (HyperText Markup Language) is a universal language used to create Web pages. It allows a document to be correctly displayed on any screen regardless of the type of computer or terminal being used. Hypertext contains links to other documents embedded within the text. It allows the user to quickly access related text from within the document they are currently reading. Hypermedia documents contain not just text but pictures, graphics, sounds, and even animation. Dedicated HTML authoring tools include Adobe PageMill and Microsoft FrontPage.

Web Browsers Made Surfing the Net Popular

The development of Web browser programs has led to the great surge in popularity of Web surfing by providing a simple way to navigate the Web by clicking on links using the mouse. It's the reason there are so many cybersurfers. An important aspect of the browser is the ease with which it can be extended to add players for sound, viewers for graphic files, and what seems to be an unending list of exciting new applications for various purposes. The line between the Internet and the Web is increasingly blurred as more and more Internet tools (software programs) are added to browsers. Browsers now allow you to access FTP (file transfer protocol) and Gopher servers and are starting to offer e-mail.

Two of the major browsers are Netscape's Navigator and Microsoft's Internet Explorer. Both companies are actively adding new personnel to support their rapid growth and to help them extend their range of services. Both companies list job offerings on their Web pages:

| Netscape | *http://www.netscape.com* |
| Microsoft | *http://www.microsoft.com* |

The newest browser, called the hyperbolic tree browser, allows a Web user to see the whole link structure of thousands of pages on a Web site all at once. Developed by InXight which is 80 percent owned by Xerox, it exploits human perceptual abilities by using graphics and animation to help make sense of large amounts of information.

Search Engines Help People Find Information

The Internet is growing so fast and in so many different directions at once that any attempt to list its resources is doomed to failure. Search engines, using the Web browser interface, allow Web users to find the information they seek, whether it is a company that sells teddy bears or a government document. Many commercial search engines make the research job easier by offering reviews and commentary. Popular commercial search engines include:

Yahoo!	*http://www.yahoo.com*
Lycos	*http://www.lycos.com*
WebCrawler	*http://www.webcrawler.com*

A Company Profile: Yahoo!

Yahoo! began in April 1994 as a way for two college students to keep track of their favorite Web sites. David Filo and Jerry Yang were Ph.D. candidates in electrical engineering at

Stanford University. They designed a customized database and developed software to help them find material on the Internet. Yahoo! is a catalog of Internet sites compiled from information submitted by users. This process differs from the Lycos engine, which searches the Internet and then catalogs what it finds. The San Jose *Mercury News* noted that "Yahoo! is closest in spirit to the work of Linnaeus, the eighteenth-century botanist whose classification system organized the natural world."

The Yahoo! catalog at first resided on Yang's student workstation while the search engine was on Filo's computer. In early 1995, they moved their files to larger computers located at Netscape. David and Jerry eventually dropped out of their Ph.D. programs to concentrate on developing their new company, which they took public in 1996. They recently endowed a $2 million chair at Stanford, the youngest individuals to do so.

Yahoo! describes their company as a fun, creative, and exciting place to work. They offer jobs in engineering, sales, marketing, and administration. You might find the following jobs at Yahoo!

In Engineering

SOFTWARE ENGINEER, SPORTS   You will be responsible for all sports-related content on Yahoo!, such as scoreboards. You will help build and maintain an up-to-date sports Web site, serving hundreds of thousands of users. You must have a bachelor's or master's degree in computer science or equivalent and two or more years of UNIX, C/C++, Perl, HTML, and Internet-related software.

SOFTWARE ENGINEER, ADVERTISING SYSTEM   You will be responsible for building the state-of-the-art Web advertising system. You must have a bachelor's or master's degree in computer science or equivalent and four or more years of UNIX and C/C++. You must have deep knowledge of data structures and have experience in distributed systems. Experienced in large-scale systems with high level of concurrency is preferred.

In Sales

INTERACTIVE AD SCHEDULER   You will work with sales reps and advertisers. Requires a B.S. degree in computer science or business and two or more years of related experience. Excellent PC skills utilizing Excel, Photoshop, databases, and window utilities and applications such as Zip, HQX, and Binhex are essential. Also requires a solid understanding of the Internet and knowledge of HTML, UNIX, FTP. The successful candidate will be well organized, ultrareliable, and possess excellent customer service skills and follow through.

In Marketing

PRODUCER   You will be responsible for the creation and implementation of new Yahoo! sites, from project initiation through completion. Involves frequent interaction and negotiation with outside partners. Requires a B.S. degree, three to five years of experience in business development and project management, and a fascination with and great understanding of the Internet. Knowledge of HTML preferred.

PROMOTIONAL GRAPHICS/WEB DESIGNER   Use your graphic design skills on the Web to create promotional campaigns. Three or more years of graphic design experience required. Must have proficiency in Photoshop, Illustrator, Debabelizer. Knowledge of HTML is required. CGI programming experience preferred but not required. Some experience in the advertising industry preferred.

In Administration

ORDER ENTRY CLERK   You will be responsible for coordinating, reviewing, and inputting advertising insertion orders into a database. The job requires a high school diploma, or equivalent, and two or more years of order-input experience. You must have excellent data entry skills and proficiency with Excel. Requires good organizational and phone skills and ability to follow through with pending issues. General database experience required, preferably with Microsoft Access.

Working as a Programmer at a Large Company

Owen Hill works as a programmer for Pacific Bell. Although he received his undergraduate degree in finance and has an M.B.A. in international business, Owen was trained by Pacific Bell as a programmer. He is currently undertaking extensive training in client server application development. Owen works to support an established Pacific Bell client server application and is assisting a new project that will mechanize a testing process utilizing Java, PYTHON, C++, VB 4.0, and other development tools.

Owen and his team use the Internet to stay current with technology as it relates to the software tools they use. This technology can change on a daily if not hourly basis. He feels that the Internet is the primary source for this information because it is constantly available and can be focused specifically on his needs. Newsgroups, chat rooms, and MSDN also offer effective ways to gain support from experienced users. Owen reports that there are simply not enough students coming out of schools with a background in client server development tools and concepts.

Career Opportunities in Programming

In the future, Owen sees companies like his focusing more and more on core technologies (in Pacific Bell's case, the network). In an increasingly "knowledge worker" based economy, this focus will increase the number of job opportunities for outside suppliers and their teams of contractors. Contractors currently earn between $45 and $60 per hour, depending on their experience. Consultants can earn $50 to $150 per hour providing what is little more than proper project management of an application or Web site development.

Network support requirements in the future will be huge. Owen sees a continued demand for electrical engineers, network designers, and server administrators. Database administrators, low-level programmers (they get down to the bits and bytes using languages such as C++), and help desk support will also be needed. Trainers in all categories for both software and hardware will be in demand, too.

Working as a Programmer to Develop New Technologies

Michael Killianey is a software engineer working for WebTV. The software he writes resides inside a box that connects a TV to the Internet. The box is basically an Internet browser that is also capable of offering e-mail and other services. He both writes the code and works on upgrades to the system. He finds it exciting that his company was virtually unknown and in six months became the defacto industry leader.

When Michael first started working for WebTV, it was a small firm with only twenty or thirty employees. Everyone worked closely together and did a little bit of everything. Now that the company has nearly two hundred employees, everyone has a more precise job description. Michael finds that with thirty or forty people who do similar things, the opportunity to learn from each other is greater.

Michael has a liberal arts degree in an interdisciplinary major and a master's degree in computer science. He paid for his education by teaching computer science classes and tutoring students in math, which he calls "a beautiful discipline." His first job was with an artificial intelligence firm doing work for the government. It only lasted three weeks. He found he was working an exact forty-hour week and having to account for his time in fifteen-minute increments. Now Michael comes to work whenever he feels ready to be productive, at 8:00 A.M. one day and 11:00 A.M. the next. He notes that you can't always think of a creative way to solve a problem at work; you may be at home cooking dinner when an idea strikes. What's important is not the number of hours, but the amount of work you get done.

After his government job, Michael developed video games for Rocket Science Games. He worked on "full-motion video," which gives an experience similar to watching a movie and playing a video game at the same time. He has been with his current firm, WebTV, for almost two years.

At its best, Michael finds that writing software allows one to create amazingly powerful solutions. When a civil engineer designs a road system, that solution is local and specific to the area. In contrast, a well-designed software solution is often generic and can be reused again and again, with minimal changes. The challenge of the Internet is that the content is always changing and new standards are continually emerging. The release of an upgrade can be awaited with the same excitement as the release of a new movie.

Software design is big business in which the best man doesn't always win. Software is in itself an abstract commodity, just a series of ones and zeros. Its value is determined by what becomes the industry standard. There are many adequate solutions in the rush to develop technology, but it is the solution that is accepted that accrues the value.

Working as a Self-Employed Programmer

John Buckman runs a small Internet software company from his home. He writes and sells software for running e-mail discussion groups on the Internet. He has written a program, TILE, which converts Lotus Notes databases to HTML and which has attracted a number of major customers. TILE allows you to easily create WWW sites from databases. It also allows users to browse the database by any number of categories.

John started working when he was fourteen as an intern at Yale University doing menial computer work. He moved up to being a programmer at the Yale University HMO during high school and college summers. He got a bachelor's degree in philosophy from Bates College and a master's in philosophy from the Sorbonne. After college, he went to work at a "futures-oriented think tank" for a year and then spent a year as a general computer consultant with a small consulting firm. After one and a half years as a programmer at the Discovery Channel, he started his own company and has been self-employed ever since.

After working on his own for several years, John says that he can never go back to working for someone else. He works seven days a week, typically from 9:00 A.M. to 11:00 P.M. with about three hours of break time during the day. Mostly he programs, although he also talks to clients over the telephone and very occasionally gives sales presentations. He spends about three hours a day answering e-mail.

John finds that self-pacing is both extremely difficult and extremely important. The challenges are mostly psychological in that it is easy to get depressed when things are not going well, and this can allow you to fall into a self-defeating slump. John initially had a difficult time with the traditional business aspects, such as accounts receivable, contracts, and taxes; but he notes that these things tend to sort themselves out over time.

John says that he sees a lot of shoddy work on the Internet, even from big companies. He believes that this presents a great opportunity for talented entrepreneurs who do quality work because they can effectively compete with huge companies, and the potential payoffs are great. The one recommendation he makes is never to show poor-quality work to the public. Because the Internet is so intangible, all that people have to base their opinions on is the quality of your work. Make sure that everything the public sees is top-notch. If you're not a graphic designer, don't do your own Web site; find a talented friend to do it for you. For more information about John, look at ***http://tile.net/john.***

Job Outlook for Programmers

As computer usage expands, the demand for skilled programmers will increase. Organizations will seek new applications and improvements to the software already in use. Employment may not grow as rapidly as in the past because improved software and programming techniques continue to simplify programming tasks. Firms will desire programmers who develop a technical specialization in areas such as client/server programming, multimedia technology, graphic user interface, or fourth- and fifth-generation programming tools. People who want to become programmers can enhance their chances by combining work experience with the appropriate formal training.

At the present time, there is a tremendous demand for programmers, expecially in the Silicon Valley area of California and in the Northeast. Firms are literally hiring programmers away from other firms. It is not unusual for a qualified programmer to start at $50,000 per year and for exceptionally skilled programmers to earn as much as $150,000 per year. Salaries will be less in other areas of the country.

CHAPTER FIVE

Helping Companies Get on the Net

A s the use of the Internet in homes, offices, businesses, government, and other organizations becomes more and more popular, companies are literally jumping aboard the Net for a variety of reasons. Some companies simply want their stockholders, customers, and employees to think that they are associated with the latest technology. An ever-increasing number want to advertise, market, or sell their products and services using this new medium. Others want to put information about their companies online to attract investors and customers and to describe employment opportunities. Whatever the reason, this avalanche of companies coming aboard the Net means jobs for cybersurfers who can help the companies become active players on the Internet. There are jobs in marketing, advertising, sales, and consulting as well as jobs in more technical areas such as providing the necessary hardware, software, and programming, which were discussed in the preceding two chapters. These jobs are being filled by company employees and independent contractors and consultants.

Internet Presence Providers

Large organizations have information systems departments that oversee the operation of their Internet activities. Nevertheless, most organizations will probably use outside professional services at times. Both large and small businesses often use the services of Internet presence providers (IPPs). An IPP can design, host, and maintain a Web site. Hosting encompasses providing computer services and Internet access connections. Maintenance includes the full-time supervision of the server, software, and hardware as well as the monitoring of the number of "hits" (times that the Web site is visited). In addition, IPPs offer the necessary technical help to build Web sites and the marketing and advertising savvy to promote the business on the Net. They also assist companies in registering domain names with the Internet Network Information Center (InterNIC), a data and directory service. Companies such as USWeb, Internet Business Solutions, and America Online's Prime Host provide these services in all-inclusive packages, while other companies and independent contractors and consultants may concentrate on providing just one or a limited number of services.

Web Site Design Services

Instead of using an Internet presence provider, companies can have their Web sites designed by a professional design firm such as Digital Planet or by one of the thousands of Web designers offering this service. The companies will then use an Internet service provider to host their site. Most large service providers, such as Netcom and UUNet, offer hosting services.

For businesses that want to go it alone, there are a variety of tools available, including Microsoft's Merchant Server. Software such as Netscape's Navigator Gold and Microsoft's

Internet Assistant are designed to make it easier to program in HTML for the company or individual building a Web site.

Cybermalls

Cybermalls are electronic versions of shopping malls, and there are many malls for online shoppers. The malls host Web sites for merchants, provide the equipment and phone lines they need, and offer marketing, site maintenance, and security. The merchants may pay a monthly rental fee or a percentage of their sales to the mall owner for the privilege of having a store at the mall. Often, just like land-based malls, cybermalls are based around a large department store that is the initial draw for attracting customers. Internet mall shoppers are generally an upscale clientele who tend to make purchase decisions quickly. As malls achieve the ability to offer secure ordering services through credit-card encryption, they will grow to their full potential. You can find jobs with cybermalls as they need technical, marketing, sales, and business people to set up and promote the mall stores.

Dave Taylor and The Internet Mall

In 1994, Dave Taylor created The Internet Mall (*http://www.internet-mall.com*). Today, they are busy continuing to grow the world's largest online shopping site. Dave is also in the process of creating what he calls a very slick, secure commerce service, OrderEasy. Dave is a very knowledgeable cybersurfer. He has a bachelor's degree in computer science and a master's in educational computing and has written four books, including *Creating Cool Web Pages with* HTML and *The Internet Business Guide*, with Rosalind Resnick.

Dave splits his time between The Internet Mall and his consulting company, Intuitive Systems (*http://www.intuitive.com*).

His principal challenge is to get things out and working in "Internet time" while still having the appearance of a life. Dave sees the Internet as a great liberator intellectually because suddenly things can be created and brought online very quickly. He says the problem, of course, is that because it can be done quickly, suddenly it *must* be done quickly, and that's anathema to quality and careful design.

Dave says that it is important to realize that the people with successful online careers are those who have good communication skills. He believes that there is really no substitute for good reading and writing ability. Writing is equally important as reading because whether you're designing a Web page, adding your two cents worth to an online discussion, or programming a Java applet, it's all about communication between you and your intended audience.

Where the Jobs Are

Visit the following Web sites for more information on Internet hosting and Web design services. Most of the sites include current job offerings.

- Microsoft's Merchant Server *http://www.microsoft.com/ merchant/partners/partner1.htm*

- Netscape's Navigator Gold
  http://home.netscape.com/

- Prime Host, a division of America Online
  http://www.primehost.com/offer/aolwelcome/compu

- USWeb is a national firm with nearly fifty franchise offices
  http://www.USWeb.com

- Online Advertising Discussion List
  http://www.tenagra.com/online_ads

- I/Pro Research specializes in marketing and advertising
  http://www.ipro.com

- Digital Planet
  http://www.digiplanet.com

Careers in Marketing and Advertising

Marketing and advertising managers work together to promote a firm's products and services. Part of this promotion is now being done on the Internet, so individuals with expertise in this new field are finding jobs with marketing and advertising firms and as consultants.

Marketing managers determine the demand for a company's products and services and identify potential consumers. These managers develop pricing strategies, monitor trends that indicate the need for new products and services, and oversee product development. Advertising managers oversee the account services, creative services, and media services departments. Marketing and advertising managers often work long hours, including evenings and weekends. Working under pressure is unavoidable as schedules change, problems arise, and deadlines and goals must be met.

Salaries start at about $22,000 for advertising managers and at about $25,000 for marketing managers. Experienced managers earn about $44,000, while the top 10 percent of managers earn more than $98,000. Surveys show that salary levels vary substantially, depending upon the level of managerial responsibility, length of service, and the size and location of the employer.

An Interactive Marketing Manager

Marvin Chow is the interactive marketing manager at Reebok International. He is responsible for all of the interactive ventures of the brand, including Web site and online development strategy, CD-rom production, and digital kiosk work. He uses the Internet for research, content and development ideas, and references.

Marvin, who has a bachelor's degree in marketing and computer science, believes that the following skills and abilities are necessary in order to be a good marketing manager:

- Technical and marketing background and understanding

- Skills to oversee project development

- Ability to communicate the creative visions of your brand

- Ability to convey technical innovations and possibilities to those of a nontechnical background

- Ability to interact with people from all backgrounds

- Visionary attitude about the future of this new technology

Marketing and the Internet

Marvin believes that the Internet breathes life into many senior marketing professionals because of its communication abilities and global reach. It is this ability to deliver energy and enthusiasm to the profession that Marvin enjoys most about his work. The downsides of his job include long hours (anywhere from sixty to ninety hours a week), occasional frustration in explaining the technicalities of the Net, and a lack of recognition by those who don't understand the new medium.

Marvin believes that the Internet will evolve into a total marketing medium similar to print or broadcast. The interactive and online media will begin to integrate into the marketing mix along with public relations, advertising, and retail merchandising. With the emergence of fully integral advertising agencies, the need for interactive managers, like Marvin, will become more critical.

An Expert in Providing Online Marketing Solutions

Before Daniel Janal launched his career as an Internet consultant, he was an award-winning newspaper reporter and business news editor and had worked in public relations. His main job today is to advise clients on how to market on the Net. Through his experience in public relations, he definitely knows what works and what doesn't. He finds that many companies have unrealistic expectations about the ways in which Net marketing can help their businesses. Daniel gives them options about what to do when they don't know what to do.

His firm, Janal Communications, works with clients from Reader's Digest to small mom-and-pop operations that want to reach online audiences. This may involve designing an online contest, publicizing a Web site, doing market research, doing competitive analysis, or planning and creating marketing materials. Daniel typically works with his clients and then goes on the Internet to do research. In the future, he believes companies will be spending more time on marketing than on the technical aspects of the Internet.

Internet Consultants

Eventually, every company is likely to have an online presence and to use that presence in some way to market a product or service. Besides the individuals mentioned previously, many companies use the services of consultants to help them gain a presence and to use the Net wisely. Sometimes, these consultants will help them choose the companies or individuals that a firm needs to get online successfully. At other times, they may perform a specific task that employees do not have the time or expertise to handle.

Obviously, consultants have to be Net savvy; they may also need to have strong technical, financial, business, marketing, library, or advertising skills. There are literally thousands of Internet consultants working with clients in one-time or long-term relationships. How much consultants earn depends upons their skills as well as their ability to find clients. Some will earn as much as $100,000 a year.

An Internet Consultant's Story

Margaret Riley brings her expertise as a librarian, Webmaster, and creator of the Riley Guide (an online job resources guide described in Chapter 1) to her work as an Internet consultant specializing in employment and recruiting services online. While working as a circulation/computer resources librarian, her reputation as an expert in online job searching began to grow as she built a solid following of career counselors. Soon she was being asked to do outside seminars and got a lot of speaking engagements. When outside work began to conflict more and more with her job as a librarian, she decided to take her chances and become a consultant.

Margaret currently has two major consulting contracts and does similar work for both clients, namely creating Internet resource libraries for the use of their clients to aid in the job search and information retrieval process. She has also worked with both clients to design or redesign existing Web servers to be more navigable and to include new information and resources.

Margaret also spends a tremendous amount of time doing presentations for career counselors and job search counselors on using the Internet. She does not work with job seekers but concentrates on working with the counselors and trainers who work with them. In order to provide her clients with the services they require, Margaret spends about six hours a day online, looking at employment and recruiting services and evaluating them—an appealing task for a cybersurfer.

Requisite Skills

In order to handle her job as a consultant, Margaret believes that certain skills are absolutely fundamental:

- the ability to teach
- the ability to present information in a way that is easy for all users to understand
- the ability to create a flow of information that is logical
- the ability to negotiate between systems developers and programmers and users

She also feels that it is essential for consultants to be enthusiastic about their work.

Additional Career Opportunities

Another career area some cybersurfers may wish to explore is operating a Web farm, which is like a cybermall but does not provide as many support services. There are also jobs for illustrators who know how to create imaginative Web pages. Market researchers are also needed to determine Internet demographics—that is, to find out just who is on the Net, what sites they are visiting, and what products they are purchasing. A need is also developing for salespeople to sell advertising space on the Net. The more the Internet takes off and every company feels that is must have an online presence, the more new job areas will continue to develop for individuals wanting to help companies become solid players on the Net.

CHAPTER SIX

Working as a Webmaster

W ebmasters are like the captains of ships and the ring masters at circuses—they are in charge of everything. Their responsibility is the day-to-day operation of Web sites. It is the Webmaster who makes sure it all happens. Here are the duties of a Webmaster:

- Coordinate and evaluate Web development projects.

- Understand the company's goals. Work with marketing to be sure the Web site is directed toward the target audience.

- Have an understanding of design and be able to implement the work of a graphics artist.

- Evaluate and implement Web tools and technology.

- Monitor Web traffic and determine bandwidth requirements.

- Maintain and monitor Web site security.

There are more than thirty million Web pages for surfers to visit on the Internet, so it is very important for companies and individuals to have distinctive and well-run sites. The Webmaster is the person who creates the public image for companies and individuals on the Net. Some Web sites will incorporate the latest in graphics and multimedia technology in an effort to capture the fleeting attention of the sophisticated cybersurfer. This type of site is frequently used by businesses attempting to sell a product on the Internet. Other sites may be less flashy, offering efficiency in the form of faster links. But regardless of the type of Web site, the overall design, content, ease of use, and quality of graphics will determine the public perception of the company or individual the site represents. Companies are increasingly recognizing the importance of the Webmaster in projecting their online presence.

Successful Web sites are the result of efforts by a diverse group of people, often working as a team. A typical group in a large company might include a marketing director, a technical manager, a content manager, a public relations specialist, a graphics designer, and a Webmaster. It is the Webmaster, however, who puts it all together.

The description of a Webmaster's job will depend on the company where he or she works. Also, the title of Webmaster is not used at all companies. What follows is a closer look at the responsibilities of four Webmasters working at quite diverse companies.

Consulting for a Hardware Company

Jeff Meador is a consultant whose client is the technical department at Hewlett-Packard, where he acts as a senior technical leader. On a typical day, he spends much of his time at meetings and on the telephone, working to make sure the Web site is developing in the way the company wants. Jeff does considerable hand-holding because so many people at the company need to understand how the Net can best work for them. He feels that it is important to keep a high level of personal contact and enjoys the time that he spends educating others about the Net.

A typical company Web site will need to be updated with new information two or three times a week. Press releases, product introductions, and rebate offers are commonly added to the site. While Jeff is responsible for the technical aspects, he may require an HTML programmer and a graphics artist to assist him.

Jeff is a true cybersurfer who spends a great deal of time surfing around the World Wide Web just to see what is out there. In order to be able to implement new Web technologies, he needs to see what is available. He finds that some new technology offers a flashy, high-end spectacle but may not add content to a Web site. Jeff believes that people would rather have informative sets of pages. Jeff also surfs the Internet in order to keep a close eye on what Hewlett-Packard's competitors are doing.

Dynamic Web publishing really excites Jeff, who has worked on a Hewlett-Packard site using this technology. Dynamic Web publishing, also called interactive programming, creates Web pages that are based on information provided by the user. No two users see the same series of pages. For example, if you wanted to find a printer ribbon, you could access a Web site selling computer equipment. By entering the make and model of printer that you are using, the Web site could then show you only the ribbons appropriate for your printer.

Jeff works at Hewlett-Packard two or three days a week. He has no set hours but typically works an eight-hour day. When Jeff works at home, he generally works from 8:00 A.M. to 11:30 A.M. and then takes a break to go to the gym and to have lunch. He works after lunch and again at night. Jeff says that he gets more done if he works at home, but that "if you work at home, you are always at work." He feels that independent work requires an enormous amount of self-discipline and would not recommend it for everyone. When Jeff worked at home exclusively before starting at Hewlett-Packard, he needed to make an effort to develop a life outside of his job.

A Look at Jeff's Background

Jeff got an early start with computers, first playing and then designing his own games. His father drafted him for computer help, and in the process Jeff learned how to set up a smoothly functioning office. In college, he took two computer programming classes. When Jeff was asked to be a teaching assistant for a class in music history, he made a multimedia presentation for each class that was so successful that he was asked to assist with a literature of fantasy class taught over the Web. This work inspired Jeff to start his own business specializing in presentation consulting and the multimedia environment on the Internet after graduating from Stanford University with a degree in American studies. About a year later, Jeff began consulting for Hewlett-Packard while still maintaining his own business.

Jeff would like to remain self-employed and to expand his company into a full agency. He says that while it is easy to get a business started, it is also easy to fall behind and that this career choice is more work than you might imagine. His best business assets, according to Jeff, are his ability to remain flexible and to work with people on a personal level.

Working for a Telephone Company

Rhonda Davis is a personnel manager for Pacific Bell. She holds a B.S. degree in math and computer science and also has an M.B.A. One of the challenges of her job is to get Pacific Bell's Web page up and running and to make sure that it is both interesting and easy to use. Working with the Web gives her both the ability to be creative and the freedom to design new processes. Rhonda will soon have an Internet recruiting manager on her team who will have the primary responsibility of sourcing from the Internet as well as posting Pacific Bell jobs on the Internet. Rhonda sees a need for future Internet workers in these areas:

- MARKETING: Continual development and enhancement of market analysis and strategies

- SALES: Development and enhancement of sales strategies

- TECHNICAL: Development of new and innovative Web pages, development of Java applications, and maintenance of Web pages

- TEACHING: Helping others use the Internet for research

Working for a Construction Company

Doug LeBlanc works as an information technology consultant for Granite Construction Company, a national company specializing in heavy construction. He is responsible for division network design, management and support; the division Web site design (*www.gcco.com*), management and maintenance; and the initial corporate Web site (*http://www.graniteconstruction.com*).

Doug's background includes a B.S. in engineering with a minor in math. Initially self-taught in computer programming, Doug has acquired certificates in graphics design, expert systems/artificial intelligence/virtual reality, and CAD/3D design. He also has attended seminars in Internet/network design and operation. Additionally, Doug holds a fine arts certificate and has studied watercolor painting, which has been a bonus in boosting his Webmaster design skills. Doug offers a look at the challenges, frustrations, and rewards of his job.

The Challenges

- Maintaining an efficient operating status for a diverse population of Internet/Intranet users

- Planning and providing tools and equipment while anticipating growth and changes in hardware and software

- Coordinating division network operation with corporate mainframe operation

The Downsides

- Complexity of validating return on investment for network and computer costs in both purchases and operation

- Solving compatibility problems of poorly written operating environments and software, magnified by constant new versions and upgrades

- Having to be cool when dealing with multiple requests that individually have an emergency status to each user

Positive Aspects

- Acknowledgment by users of increased efficiency in their work

- The timeliness and efficiency of e-mail

- Feeling like a "crafty wizard" when defeating a computer glitch

Working for a Publisher

Michael McCulley is a Webmaster within the Mar-Com group for Knight-Ridder Information. Michael works on the Web server, on the Web site, and with design and layout requirements. It is his job to edit, update, change, design, and prepare HTML and code pages for the Web site. He is also involved with marketing and promoting new products, services, and publication. He works with product managers, sales staff, and technical staff and spends about three hours every day on the Internet.

Michael holds a bachelor's degree in English and a master's in librarianship. He became involved with the Internet while he was working as a librarian at UC San Diego. Michael says that keeping up with the ever-changing Internet landscape is critical for Webmasters. There are always new options to be developed which is high pressure but fun in a challenging way. To keep abreast of changes in technology, he reads e-mail and mailing lists and uses the Web daily. He says it is a great place for a librarian to be working.

Michael lists these skills as a valuable mix for anyone interested in an Internet career:

- EDITORIAL SKILLS: journalism

- BUSINESS SAVVY: marketing and communications

- TECHNICAL SKILLS: not just programming, but understanding how the parts work together

- WEB KNOWLEDGE: knowing what's there, what's being done

What It Takes to Be a Webmaster

If you are planning a career as a Webmaster, you will find that many jobs require specific technical skills. Additionally, almost all companies stress good communication skills and the ability to work well with people, as a Webmaster most often works as part of a team. When looking for a Webmaster position, you might find that the following skills and responsibilities are required:

Entry-Level Web Programmer

SKILLS REQUIRED:

- Skill in Perl programming
- Familiarity with Unix, preferably Solaris
- Understanding of HTML, HTTP, CGI, SSI, and JavaScript
- Understanding of basic shell scripting
- Knowledge of C++ or Java

RESPONSIBILITIES:

- Write CGI scripts to process forms from the Web
- Write scripts to convert various text files to HTML
- Assist the Web designer to redesign sections of the site
- Create daily maintenance scripts (e.g. archiving)
- Help the Web designer in adding JavaScript to the site

Web Designer

SKILLS REQUIRED:

- Experience in Web/database design
- Knowledge of HTML

- Strong communication skills

- Ability to work in a team environment

RESPONSIBILITIES:

- Monitor Web traffic

- Produce statistical reports

- Determine bandwidth requirements

- Maintain and monitor Web site security

- Advise and coordinate Web development projects

- Evaluate and implement Web tools and technology

Senior Web Manager

SKILLS REQUIRED:

- Bachelor's degree in computer science or related field

- Significant Web management experience

- Application design experience

RESPONSIBILITIES:

- Develop and lead a team in building a Web site

- Develop, implement, and maintain Web site for customer support, sales support, direct sales, and company news

- Design server platform and network

- Maintain Web site security

The Pay Scale for Webmasters

Pay levels for Webmaster positions vary widely and depend somewhat on the size of the company offering the position as well as on the skill levels and responsibilities required. Average salary for an experienced Webmaster is about $55,000 per year. Entry-level Webmasters can earn between $25,000 and $35,000, while a few top-level Webmasters earn more than $95,000.

The Webmaster's Guild

The Webmaster's Guild was founded in 1995 to educate, promote, and unify the Webmaster community. It provides an active forum for Web professionals to share information within and across all Web disciplines. Go to the Guild's Web site at *http://www.webmaster.org* to learn more about the organization and about a career as a Webmaster. The Guild puts on events for members, runs online discussion groups so members can have an opportunity to communicate, and has a reading list for Webmasters. It also offers seminars to train people to become Webmasters.

CHAPTER SEVEN

Providing a Unique Service on the Internet

One reason the Internet is growing so fast is because it has so many practical uses. Do you want a job? The Net has more job listings than any newspaper. Would you like to take a college course without leaving your home? Several universities have online classrooms. Are you curious about your bank balance? Your bank may offer online banking services. Are you bored and looking for entertainment? You can play a game on the Net with someone across the country or find out what is showing at a local movie theater. Would you like to buy a plane ticket or rent a car? You can do it on the Internet. The number of unique services that you can find on the Internet is expanding in many imaginative ways. Here are just a few examples of the hundreds of services you can now access on the Net:

medical advice	movie reviews
weather reports	horoscopes
hotel reservations	passport applications
traffic reports	college catalogs
insurance quotes	sports news and scores
sightseeing information	parenting tips

legal advice   art galleries

book reviews   tax forms

census information   bithday reminders

maps   beauty tips

Employment Opportunities

A wide range of jobs exists in the service arena on the Net. Web sites need to be built, maintained, and updated, which means jobs for programmers, Webmasters, Web designers, HTML coders, technical assistants, and database architects, to name just a few jobs. You don't have to be a technical whiz, however, to work closely with the Internet. Customer service representatives, trainers, librarians, researchers, editors, writers, and human relations and public relations department workers spend much of their workday on the Net. This chapter will introduce you to just a few of the areas where you can now find jobs. Surf the Net frequently, and you will find many more innovative services.

Jobs in Financial Services

No longer do people have to visit a bank or brokerage firm; now they can turn their homes into branch banks and buy stocks and bonds using the Internet. Few people are now availing themselves of these unique services; however, this will rapidly change as people begin to learn how much easier online financial services can make their lives. Many Internet researchers believe that financial services will become one of the most popular services offered on the Internet.

Online Banking

A new breed of banks is rapidly emerging. In 1995 only 20 percent of the banks with assets less than $300 million offered PC-based online services, while 80 percent of the banks with $5 billion or more offered these services, according to the American Bankers Association. By 2001 most banks will offer some online services. Large corporations already conduct many of their transactions electronically, and it is expected that smaller firms and residential customers will also jump on the online banking bandwagon.

Wells Fargo Bank

Over one hundred years ago, Wells Fargo stagecoaches traveled across the American West delivering mail and cash. Today the bank is one of the leaders in offering online banking service through the Internet, America Online, Prodigy, Quicken, and Microsoft Money. Consumers can pay bills to anyone in the United States using any one of these channels. They may also view their account information and transfer money between their Wells Fargo checking, savings, credit card, line of credit, and money market mutual fund accounts. Customers using the Internet can then download account history for their personal checking, savings, and credit card accounts. Furthermore, merchants can accept online payments for the goods and services they sell over the Internet with help of Wells Fargo's secured Internet electronic payment service. Wells Fargo first offered online banking in 1989 and Internet services in May 1995.

Wells Fargo has more than three hundred employees supporting their online business. There are approximately seventy-five professionals who handle marketing, systems development, channel management, and operational management. The other employees handle customer service of the online business. Cybersufers can go aboard the Net at **http://wellsfargo.com** to view employment opportunities for such positions as product manager, senior applications programmer/analyst, Web site manager, technical support supervisor, marketing manager, and many others.

Online Trading and Investing

Changes are brewing in the financial market. Ever since investors became cybersurfers, they have gone online at thousands of Web sites to get information and advice that once was only available from a broker or to professional investors. On the Net, investors were able to get market quotes, analyses, and predictions and participate in discussion forums. Late in 1995, cybersurfers had the additional opportunity to buy and sell stocks, securities, and mutual funds. Acceptance of online trading and investing was so rapid that by the end of 1996 there were an estimated 1.5 million online brokerage accounts. It is expected that the number of these accounts will be close to ten million by 2001. Here is one area of the Net where the opportunity to make money for providing a service is golden. The competition for business will be fierce as new start-ups come online as well as traditional brokerage houses. With the growth in online investing, the number of jobs for cybersurfers at brokerage firms will rapidly increase.

E*Trade

E*Trade is considered the pioneer of online brokerage firms. Not only does the firm offer investors the opportunity to trade via the Net, it also lets them trade through America Online, CompuServe, a direct modem connection, and touch-tone telephone. E*Trade offers a range of portfolio management tools and access to company research, market analysis, news, and other information services twenty-four hours a day, seven days a week. Click on "Employment Opportunities" at the main menu to see the responsibilities and qualifications for Internet-related jobs at E*Trade (*http://www.etrade.com*). You might find positions like the following:

Department   Customer Service

Position   Customer Service Representatives

Responsibilities   In this position, you will be responsible for providing the brokerage expertise needed to ensure that our C/S team meets its departmental goals, while providing a high level of customer satisfaction. Responding to a high volume of calls, you will provide clients with a variety of account, product, procedural, and systems information assistance.

Qualifications   The position requires education or training equivalent to a B.A./B.S. degree, preferably in business administration, finance, or related field; six months or greater prior customer service experience, preferably in a call-center environment; and a willingness to learn the securities business, along with excellent communication, analytical, time management, and organizational skills. PC proficiency and the ability to multitask and prioritize responsibilities is essential. Series 7/63 license highly desirable. Online (Internet, AOL, etc.) literacy preferred. Ability to work flexible shift assignments is required.

Department   Applications Development

Position   HTML Coder

Responsibilities   E*Trade is looking for individuals to work with our Internet development group. The successful candidate must have strong experience with HTML scripting and Web page development. Knowledge of CGI scripting, Perl, or Java would be a big plus.

QUALIFICATIONS Working with our Internet development and marketing groups, you will make changes to our Web site through the use of HTML scripting. You will also have an opportunity to work with CGI and Perl. Knowledge of software documentation is helpful in this position. This would be an excellent position for a student majoring in computer science or some other computer-related field.

Online Employment Services

Job hunting using the Internet has really taken off and is rapidly changing how professional, managerial, and technical people look for work. This trend should continue as most of today's college students actually have an Internet address and spend several hours online each week. The Internet is also changing the way that unskilled workers find jobs as the government employment agencies in almost every state now have huge lists of job openings online for positions from fast-food workers to assembly-line workers. Furthermore, a national job market is being created as access to the Internet is letting job seekers find jobs in every state.

Companies with online job sites had revenues of $4 million in 1996. By 2001, it is projected that their revenues will dramatically jump to more than $300 million, which should mean a substantial increase in the number of workers in these companies.

JobTrak—An Online Job Listing Service

JobTrak, at **http://www.jobtrak.com**, is a unique service that lets students and alumni of more than five hundred colleges look at job listings online at no cost. In 1996 more than 500,000 job openings were posted on the service. On the Web site, students and young alumni can also work on their resumes, find out how to negotiate a salary, or prepare for an interview. JobTrak creates partnerships with college placement centers and allows employers to target their job listings to any or all of the more than five hundred member campuses nationwide. More than 250,000 employers have used JobTrak, paying a small fee per campus per listing.

When Ken Ramberg graduated from college in 1987, he saw firsthand the inefficiency in the way employers had to post job listings separately to different universities. Along with two partners, he started JobTrak in 1988 as a central data processing center that transmitted job listings to colleges via modem for storage on each university's local PC database. With the advent of the Internet, JobTrak develped a Gopher system to access the database and then went aboard the World Wide Web when it became available. Today, most major university career centers have teamed up with JobTrak to process job listings and make them available to their job seekers both via the Web and in hard copy. In 1992 JobTrak was honored as the Entrepreneur of the Year by the State of California. In the future, Ken sees employers moving away from newspapers to the Internet to post job listings as they can include far more information.

The Jobs at JobTrak

When JobTrak started, the company had four employees. One was a programmer and the rest were out trying to get business. Today, there are more than eighty-five employees, which illustrates how rapidly these companies are growing. Besides top management and office and human resources managers, JobTrak has five very young full-time programmers—all in their twenties. Two were originally hired as interns. The programmers integrate the database with the Net, which requires them to keep abreast of the latest technological changes. There are three trainers who work with the customer service employees teaching them to do basic troubleshooting, which involves answering questions about the Web site and helping students and alumni navigate the Net and do resumes. The customer service employees, who need to have a broad knowledge of the Internet, are also taught how to take phone listings and enter them into the database. The other employees are two staffers who work in college relations and visit college career centers demonstrating JobTrak and trying to bring aboard new colleges.

Services Directly Associated with the Internet

New services are constantly emerging to enhance the use of the Internet. It is now possible to have Web sites monitored day and night to ensure that they are operating as they were designed. Free e-mail service is being offered by several small companies, and e-mail messages can be sent anonymously through remailers. Furthermore, it is possible to read e-mail messages on pagers and hear them on phones and to have faxes redistributed online. You can also have content delivered directly from the Internet to your computer. Most of the companies providing these services are small and are created and staffed by people in their twenties who are fascinated by the Internet.

WebPatrol—A Web Site Monitor

In 1996 WebPatrol, a part of the Allegro Group, went online with a state-of-the-art system designed to evaluate the performance of Web servers. Every fifteen minutes around the clock, customers' sites are remotely monitored and problems are immediately reported by e-mail or pager. Page retrieval time is measured and averaged each time WebPatrol accesses a customer's Web server. These statistics are automatically delivered to customers. At midnight each evening, WebPatrol requests customers' Web pages from their Web servers to verify that the pages have not been moved or edited without the customers' knowledge. All of these services are vital if a customer's sole source of income is the Web pages. The president of the Allegro Group describes WebPatrol as a fun project that involved a lot of hard work and effort to set up. The average age of the employees is twenty-four. Within WebPatrol, there are jobs in technical support that involve answering the phone and e-mail and helping customers with difficulties, and there are jobs for people who do software development. These programmers must know how to write software that communicates with and around the Internet. Most current programmers are self-taught. Sales and promotion for WebPatrol are handled by the general office. You can visit the WebPatrol site at *http://www.Webpatrol.com*.

Interpage Network Services—Telecommunications-Based Services

Because the Internet is such a new and dynamic organism, creative young people can have an idea, implement it, and discover that they have developed a successful company. While taking a car trip one day, Doug Reuben wondered what e-mail had arrived on his computer at home. He had a pager with him that provided information about phone calls. Doug soon came up with the idea of putting e-mail messages on pagers and fax machines, and Interpage Network Services (*http://www.interpage.net*) was born. A programmer friend, Doug Fields, became his partner and developed the necessary software to link e-mail with pagers and fax machines. Doug Reuben did administrative work at first, but publicity was important so he responded to newsgroup postings on technical communications issues relevant to the new company. He also set up links to many Web sites. The cost for starting the company was between

$15,000 and $20,000. At first, Doug and his partner gave away the new service to get customers. Once this business became established, the company saw other niches and added more services for Internet users, including an online shopping service, a site and server monitoring service, a fax mailbox, and the delivery of news, weather, stock, or personal reminders from the Web to pagers and fax machines. All of the day-to-day work of Interpage is automatic except getting and keeping customers.

Today, this fledgling company has eight employees. Besides the owners, there are two customer service representatives, two systems supervisors, a billing clerk, and a staff member to handle large accounts. In the future, Doug believes that the staff will double or triple and will include programmers. He sees the company developing into a complete communications service to businesses with all of Interpage's services oriented toward the continued integration of the Internet with traditional communications media. He would like Interpage to build strategic relationships with large telecommunications companies in order to do specialized work for them.

E-Mail Services Galore

One of the most popular and addictive of all Internet activities is e-mail. Now several small companies are offering free e-mail, and the only price is that you must agree to receive ads that are based on personal information you have supplied. Juno On-Line Services (one of the largest providers of e-mail services in the United States) now has more than 1.5 million subscribers and lets customers send and receive an unlimited number of e-mail messages anywhere in the world. Stop by Juno's employment pages at *http://www.juno.com* and you will discover that the company is looking for people to work in a variety of capacities within its New York, California, and Boston offices:

If you have a track record of outstanding accomplishment (whether in academia or the 'real' world), we'd like you to get in touch with us. We are seeking exceptional software engineers (including top-notch Windows hackers and C/Unix gurus), world-class systems wizards, experts at quality assurance and member services, marketing pros and superstar ad salespeople, as well as individuals of extraordinary ability who don't fit into any of these categories.

Webcasting—A Hot New Concept

Webcasting has taken away the need to surf for news, sports, weather, and stock information by delivering the specially tailored information customers want to their desks. Delivery can be on screen savers, on a floating ticker, or by onscreen or e-mail notification when new material arrives. And the content also has hyperlinks that can lead customers back to the Web for more information. This is an area that promises great growth. It is the start of a revolution in the way people receive information from the Internet. It's letting people have the information they want delivered to them instead of having to surf for it on the Net. Experts predict that this service will take off and generate as much as $5 billion by the turn of the century. Some of the companies now offering this new service include:

AirMedia	*http://www.airmedia.com*
Berkeley Systems	*http://www.afterdark.com*
PointCast	*http://www.pointcast.com*
Marimba	*http://www.marimba.com*

Visit the above Web sites to learn more about Webcasting and employment opportunities at these companies. On the Berkeley Systems job page, you'll be able to see the slide connecting their second and first floors. The company also has a Mortal Kombat machine in the kitchen. It can be fun to work in the cyberworld.

Online Multiplayer Games

The millions of game players who have become accustomed to playing video games now have the opportunity to play games against or with multiple players on the Internet. And besides playing games, they can enter contests and gaming competitions, chat with other players, keep track of stats in different games, and find news about games and game strategies. Analysts believe that multiplayer online gaming will become a $1 billion industry by the year 2000. This is phenomenal growth for a business that only came online in 1996. Look at the Web sites of gaming companies like Total Entertainment Network (TEN) (*http://www.ten.net*) and Mpath Interactive (*http://www.mpath.com*). You will immediately discover a need for employees, from Web site designers to Internet game hackers. There are even jobs for game testers. If you are a game designer, you may be able to sell a game to one of these companies as they will always be looking for fresh new games.

Working in the World of Online Gaming

In September 1996, TEN became the first commercial Internet entertainment network to offer nationwide high-speed multiplayer gaming. In less than four months, more than 22,000 paying subscribers registered to play TEN's hit action, strategy, simulation, and role-playing PC games. And in just a year the staff increased from 15 to 120. When you work for a growing company in an emerging market, everything is very new and turbulent.

Chairman of TEN

While in high school, Daniel Goldman played simple computer games with friends late into the night—an activity that would influence his career. He left college one unit short of a degree in physics and computer science to become an outside games developer for MAXIS, where he wrote the DOS and some Windows and Japanese versions of the popular SimCity games. His association with MAXIS lasted until 1993. During this time, he started Signum Computer Services, which focused on the creation of an online role-playing game in 1986, and Tangent Online in 1989, which ultimately evolved into TEN. His interest has always been in creating products that make it easier for people to socialize and communicate. With TEN and its interactive games and chat rooms, this goal is being reached.

As Chairman of TEN, Daniel has the job of overseeing the long-term direction of the company. He finds it exciting to be part of a new medium as it unfolds, to interact with all the bright people in this field, and to influence the direction online gaming is taking.

Editorial Director of TEN

While in college majoring in cognitive science and computer science, Chris Lombardi got a headstart on his future by working part time as an editorial assistant at *Computer Gaming World* (CGW) magazine, where he was a receptionist, subscription clerk, mailroom boy, and gofer. After graduation, he became an online projects manager assigned to bring the CGW materials to the Prodigy online service. Sadly, just as the project was going to launch, Prodigy fired a large portion of its staff, including most of the game staff, and the games area of Prodigy was never fully implemented. This was Chris's first experience of the speed with which things can change in the online world. After the Prodigy project, he became an associate editor and then eighteen months later the editor, which made him responsible for the overall "look and feel" of the magazine.

Chris left the magazine world to become the editorial director at TEN, where he has three major responsibilities:

1. *Create editorial materials related to games on the TEN service.*
   His team of six editors writes strategy and tips articles,

news about games and events on TEN, and support materials such as "Help" and "ReadMe" files.

2. *Create and administer events on the game service.* His staff develops ideas for game tournaments and contests and then works with the marketing group to make these events happen.

3. *Evaluate new games for TEN.* His team acts as the "gaming experts" for the company. Before a new game is brought onto TEN, the team makes sure it is a quality product and appropriate for online gaming.

In order to handle his responsibilities, Chris works between fifty-five and sixty-five hours a week. A lot of his time is spent on the Internet. Throughout the day, he goes onto the Web to do research, put up new editorial materials, get information from the company's Intranet, and see how things are going on the TEN site. He has continual contact with the artists and designers, the marketing team, the people who develop relationships with game companies and bring new games to TEN, and various members of the technology staff, including programmers, HTML writers, and database managers.

According to Chris, the Internet is a fascinating place to be right now. He likes being with a new company because it gives him the opportunity to do and learn things that would never be possible at a more established company and industry. On the downside, because everything is so new, things can change in an instant, and what you have worked so hard to create must often be reevaluated and changed.

Online Information Services

When professionals need to know something and to know it right away, they use information services that contain millions of documents. The three largest services are LEXIS-NEXIS (*http://www.lexis-nexis.com*), Knight-Ridder Information (*http://www.KRINFO.com*), and Dow Jones (*http://www.dowjones.com*). Their information is broad and deep and growing constantly. For example, LEXIS-NEXIS has a total of one billion documents online in 6,200 databases and adds twelve million documents each week. There are also smaller information services that tend to specialize in narrow subject areas. Many of the Internet access companies such as America Online and Prodigy also offer information to their customers. All of these companies offer a wide range of employment opportunities to match the skills and interests of cybersurfers, whether they are technical gurus who want to work with databases, systems support, or software development, or those who want to be closely involved with the Internet as customer service representatives, marketing and sales team members, or researchers. Most information services will list career opportunities on their Web pages. Here are the requirements for two positions that were listed by LEXIS-NEXIS on its Web pages.

Customer Service

DESCRIPTION Customer service representatives are available virtually twenty-four hours a day and respond to an average of five thousand calls per day. Most customer service representatives are lawyers, librarians, accountants, financial analysts, or computer analysts, and many hold M.B.A. degrees.

Search Reps provide consultative telephonic search logic support and problem resolution.

Technical Support Reps provide consultative telephonic technical support, which includes integrating, customizing, and troubleshooting LEXIS-NEXIS communication software.

EXPERIENCE Customer service job candidates must possess excellent communications skills, a strong customer service orientation, diagnostic skills, and online research skills. Customer service search reps with a paralegal degree should have two years of experience as a paralegal. Customer service technical support reps must have proven knowledge of DOS and Windows operating systems. Data communication protocols skills are a plus.

EDUCATION Candidates must have attained a degree in one or more of the following disciplines or have equivalent work experience: computer science, MIS, finance, economics, journalism, library science, paralegal, or law.

Technical

DESCRIPTION Our technology experts utilize the latest advances in software technology in a state-of-the-art development environment. Our goals are to enhance our online database technologies and provide revolutionary new products.

EXPERIENCE Technical job candidates must possess a minimum of two years of experience in software development and support and the ability to recognize and apply new software development concepts. Candidates must have experience with some of the following:

- Development in Windows, UNIX, or MVS Environments

- C, C++, Pascal, Visual C++, Visual Basic, X-Windows, Mainframe Assembler, PL/I

- SGML, HTML, SAS/SLAM

- OOA/OOD, OMT

- DCE, OLE, Powerbuilder

- JCL, TSO, ROSCOE

- PC (Intel), Sun, HP, IBM/Amdahl/HDS Mainframe

- Oracle, Sybase, Object Store, Objectivity, IDMS, DB2

- LAN, WAN, X.25, TCP/IP, FDDDI, Ethernet, ATM

EDUCATION   Candidates must have attained a degree in computer science, computer engineering, or have equivalent work experience.

Online Sports and Entertainment Services

Cybersurfers who are sports buffs or movie or television addicts should look into the job opportunities that are appearing at all the companies rushing to bring sports and entertainment to the Internet. Most radio and television stations have staked out territory on the World Wide Web. Besides news, weather, and traffic updates, they have entertainment news and frequently offer newsgroups for fans of various shows. Major movie studios are just beginning to come aboard the Internet and are primarily publicizing their films, although interactive games have been developed for such films as *Jumanji* and *Casper*. The entertainment industry is just beginning to make its presence known on the Internet and is growing by leaps and bounds. The sports world, on the other hand, has some of the most popular sites on the Web, which are drawing hundreds of thousands of visitors each day.

Sports in Cyberspace—a Cybersuccess Story

You will find more than five thousand sports-related sites operated by professional leagues, sports magazines, major media, small companies, and individuals. There are sites for every sport, from baseball to croquet to water polo. All of these sites are loaded with statistics, commentary, player information, and live chat facilities. Sports fans can access real-time scores and highlights as well as participate in fantasy games.

ESPNET SportsZone

SportsZone (***http://ESPNET.sportszone.com***) is one of the most popular sites on the net (averaging 7.5 million hits per day) and one of the leading generators of ad revenue. It offers sports news, stats, and scores updated a thousand times an hour. There is exclusive analysis from ESPN's experts, an animated look at the big plays in the NFL, weekly interactive challenges, fantasy leagues, and live audio game broadcasts. SportsZone is one of several sports and entertainment sites of Starwave Corporation. For job information, go to ***http://www.starwave.com***, where you might see a listing like this one:

Sportzone Intern

POSITION TYPE   Regular, full-time

PROJECT/DEPARTMENT   ESPNET SportsZone

REQUIREMENTS   The ideal candidate will have excellent writing skills; passion for sports; experience in sports journalism strongly preferred; knowledge of the Internet and its tools, such as the WWW and HTML; ability to work well within a team environment; text processing and video/audio production is a plus; flexible schedule.

DESCRIPTION   The SportsZone Intern will be responsible for writing and editing player profiles, transcribing audio from ESPN, compiling news and feature items, handling other duties as assigned, answering e-mail, posting scores, and compiling sports statistics.

Public Relations Assistant at Starwave

Jobs that let cybersurfers work on the Net all day are not always obvious. One of these jobs at Starwave Corporation—public relations assistant—is held by Jennifer Yazzolino. After graduation from college with a major in communication, Jennifer worked for an event company doing special events before coming to Starwave in 1995 as an administrative assistant. Now, as the only in-house public relations employee, she handles press releases, fields media calls, sets up speeches for executives, and works on public relations strategies with three outside firms. Approximately 75 percent of her workday is spent on the Net because she has to know what is out there, from company site content to articles about her company in online publications. She also has to update the corporate site to tell what is happening in the company every day, which required her to learn some HTML. Because her company is young and growing so fast, it is not uncommon for employees to become workaholics, spending fourteen to fifteen hours a day on the job—especially engineers who are constantly coming up with new applications.

Online College Courses

Students can now sit at home and take college courses online from approximately four hundred schools in the United States and Canada, with even more schools expected to come online soon. Attending cybercolleges, which can lead to a degree or certificate, is especially helpful to those who need to work full-time or live far from a college. At most schools, the entire course is conducted online. Students can enroll and order their books online, use e-mail to communicate with their teachers and fellow students, post messages on bulletin boards for other students, chat in real time with their teachers and classmates, download materials from the course's online library, and do research using Internet resources. Students don't usually have to go to colleges or designated testing centers except for final exams. Visit the Peterson's site at ***http://www.petersons.com/delearn/*** to find out more about the colleges offering online courses.

University of California

University of California Extension offers courses online via America Online. Most of the students are from California; however, some are from as far away as Singapore. By the year 2000, UC Extension expects to have 175 courses online. You can learn more about the school's online courses by looking at its World Wide Web site at ***http://www.cmil.unex.berkeley.edu/***. In order to deliver online courses, UC Extension, like other cybercolleges, employs teachers as well as technical and administrative staff. Teachers for the online program are typically University of California faculty members, faculty members from other colleges, and specialists in business and professional fields. They are selected for their interest in working individually with students at a distance. These teachers must write course materials, and to do so they must have an understanding of what it is technically possible to present online. They must know how to use e-mail, post notices on bulletin boards, and handle real-time online discussions as well as be aware of the resources on the Internet that will aid their students. In addition to academic and other specialized staff on the administrative side, there are technical experts responsible for putting the program online. These include instructional designers, graphic designers, programmers, and others who are knowledgeable about the Internet and telecommunications industries.

Online Car Buying Services

Buying a car is often a hassle with customers having to search for the vehicle they want and then engage in a prolonged haggle to get the best price. Now it is possible to find the perfect car online. Several companies let consumers search their Web sites for the desired year, make, and model of a car. Then the consumer is given the name of the dealer who has the car, eliminating the need to go from dealer to dealer.

CarSmart—Driving Business to Car Dealers

CarSmart went online at *http://www.carsmart.com* in the third quarter of 1996 to assist consumers in locating, pricing, purchasing, and leasing new or used vehicles. By January of 1997, the Web site was receiving more than twenty thousand requests a day from consumers wanting to find nearby dealers who had specific vehicles. Within hours of a request, the CarSmart dealer representative contacts the customer with the dealer's best price or lease payment on the specified vehicle. CarSmart services are free, with the exception of vehicle pricing reports.

In order to handle this business, CarSmart now has fifteen full-time employees and is looking for more. The head programmer manages the programming department, which has four support programmers. They work with very sophisticated databases and are constantly adding new features as consumers and dealers request them. An advertising analyst spends the day surfing the Internet searching for sites where the company can establish links to get more customers and looking at CarSmart's ads online. Six salespeople have the task of signing up more dealers. All have to be Internet savvy as they often show dealers how to get aboard the Net. Four dealer assistant coordinators who are able to get around in Windows process the inquiries and send them to the dealers. Three or more data-entry people are needed to update the car inventories. These entry-level employees are mostly temporary workers. The president, Michael Gorun, who was one of the founders of the service, coordinates the entire process. This job, like those at any other start-up company, requires a tremendous amount of work. Twelve-hour days are common.

A Unique Online Service—Surf Information

The successful companies providing services on the Internet are those that have found a niche that draws cybersurfers. This service niche can draw a large group such as investors, sports fans, or travelers. Or it can attract quite a small group, such as serious surfers—ocean surfers, that is. Understanding surfers' needs for surf information and forecasts led SurfLine to put comprehensive surf information on the Internet at **http:// www.surfline.com** in 1995. If you make a quick tour of the site, you will note reports describing surf conditions around the world, surf "e-lerts" offering e-mail when the surf goes off, links to surf shops, and live views of the surf from SurfLine's video cameras.

SurfLine was started in 1985 by Sean Collins and Jerry Arnold, two ardent surfers, to provide recorded surf information on the phone. They employ a network of one hundred part-time surf watchers who check the surf around the world two or three times a day and then call an area coordinator who puts the information into a script for the 900-number phone service and faxes the information to the company to update the Web site. The Internet information is free, and Sean hopes to keep it so through advertising and sponsorships.

Sean and Jerry felt that having a Web site was a natural step for their company. The site was developed by an outside company; however, the West Coast coordinators, along with a coordinator on the East Coast, do the updates. Sean and Jerry's focus now is on finding ways to make the Web site profitable. The more revenue they earn, the more video cams they hope to set up so cybersurfers can see the surf at most major beaches.

Preparing for a Job
Providing Internet Services

The first step in getting a job with a company that provides Internet services is to become "Netwise," which should be an enjoyable task for cybersurfers and other online types. No matter what your job will be, you will need to be able to navigate around the Internet and handle e-mail. The second step is to surf through the employment and jobs pages of companies that interest you to see exactly what qualifications they are seeking. While college is a prerequisite for many positions, many people have gained the required technical expertise through their own cybersurfing and computer experiences. A man who was former the janitor at a small company now maintains another company's extensive Web setup because he knew enough HTML to say, "Yes, I can do that," when he was asked for help. This happened because people think that eighteen- to twenty-five-year-olds know about computers. When you look at job ads, notice that, in addition to technical skills, most employers are looking for employees who have good oral and written communications skills and organizational skills. Here is the solid ad-

vice of a recent college graduate who has quickly climbed the
Internet corporate ladder:

Chris Lombardi of TEN:

"Breadth! Breadth! Breadth! Get as much experience in as
many areas as possible—technology, writing, project management, and art. Specialization in one field or another will get
you a good job, but it's the generalists with a broad base of
knowledge who can bring this knowledge to bear on new problems who will get to do the most interesting work. The best way
to acquire this knowledge is to learn as you earn. Get a low-
level job in an interesting company and take every opportunity
you can to learn. Keep your eyes open, talk to your manager,
volunteer for any task that will extend your experience. Always
think about your job no matter what it is in terms of the big
picture and the broader company goals. At TEN, we've had four
receptionists in the last eighteen months who have been pro-
moted into new jobs and new areas of the company—marketing, customer support, product development—because they
were smart, eager, hardworking people."

CHAPTER EIGHT

Becoming an Internet Entrepreneur

Selling Products on the Internet

T he excitement is high, and TV ads abound telling people how they can make big money selling a product on the Internet. Newspapers and magazines, as well, have fired people's interest in starting online businesses by describing the success stories of those who have made big profits selling in cyberspace. Is there a genuine opportunity to start a successful business on the Internet, or is it mostly hype?

First of all, it's important to understand that shopping on the Internet is just in its infancy—it's a business that only really started in the 1990s. Of the estimated twenty-five to thirty million people on the Net today, only 10 percent are actually making online purchases. However, the potential for far more customers is enormous, since figures as high as 250 million Internet users have been projected by the year 2001. Market research firms don't agree on how much merchandise is being sold today, but all agree that sales will skyrocket into the billions in the years ahead.

While the opportunities are decidedly there for individuals to own successful Internet businesses, there are several reality checks that future Net entrepreneurs need to make. Sales on the Internet are not booming yet. There are more browsers than shoppers in most online stores. Only a very few companies are now making a profit in cyberspace. It is not easy to establish a successful online business—knowledge, dedication, and hard work are the key ingredients.

The First Step: Learning about the Internet

If you are thinking of becoming an entrepreneur and selling a product on the Internet or would like to work for a company that does, you must have some knowledge of how the Net works. This does not mean that you must become a technical guru; however, you should be at home navigating the Net as most cybersurfers are. If you aren't, reading a book such as *The Internet for Dummies* by John R. Levine and Carol Baroudi gives Internet newcomers all the basic information needed to get started. Or you can go online at Paradesa Media (**http://www. learnthenet.com**) to learn about the Net from a very helpful tutorial on how to surf the Web. Also, it is possible to take classes or even have a private tutor to help you discover how to be a cybersurfer. Many public libraries have docent programs to teach individuals how to use the Net. Training others to use the Internet will be discussed as a career option in Chapter 9.

If you are a technical whiz, it will be easy for you to get your business online. If you aren't, there are loads of experts ready to help you. Before consulting one, read about the services you will need in such books as *101 Businesses You Can Start On The Internet* by Daniel S. Janal, *The New Internet Business Book* by Jill H. Ellsworth and Matthew V. Ellsworth, or *Making More Money on the Internet* by Alfred and Emily Glossbrenner. Or you can go aboard the Internet and ask your questions in a chat room or find more information in the previously mentioned Paradesa Media Web site.

The Second Step: Checking Out the Competition

You don't have to be a seasoned businessperson to become an entrepreneur on the Net. You could be a college student or even a high school student—many have started their own businesses. According to marketing experts, one of the biggest secrets to making money on the Net is to offer something that is unique. Instead of just selling records, Tower Records, at *http:// www.towerrecords.com*, lets prospective customers listen to sample music they're interested in before they purchase it. Besides selling their product on the Net, many companies, especially flower and gift stores, are also offering to send you an e-mail reminder of special events such as birthdays and anniversaries.

The best way for you to get an idea of all the products currently being sold on the Internet and discover what your own product niche might be is to visit an online shopping mall, also known as a cybermall. When you get to a cybermall, choose a category such as appliances, automotive, clothing, electronics, food and drink, home improvement, or sporting goods and you'll quickly discover the immense variety of items being sold in cyberspace. A visit to The Internet Mall (*http://www. internet-mall.com*), the world's largest Internet shopping mall, will give you access to more than twenty thousand Internet-based merchants. Other large general malls that you could visit include: Galaxy Mall at *http://www.galaxymall.com* and 21st Century Plaza at *http://www.21stcenturyplaza.com*.

At present, the highest sales are enjoyed by companies selling software, and this is expected to continue into the next century. Other products that are hot sales items include: books, music, travel, entertainment, home electronics, computer hardware, clothes, jewelry, and sunglasses. Look at the stores in these areas carefully. Caution: If your product will not sell in a real-world store or a catalog, it won't sell online either. You must choose a product that will appeal to your potential online customers. Typically, they are young (average age in their thirties), well-educated, and well-off, earning far more than the average U.S. salary. They are also likely to be employed in educational, computer-related, or professional or management occupations. Most of your customers will be male as only about one-third of the Net users are women.

Step Three: Acquiring Internet Marketing Savvy

Prospective entrepreneurs must understand that there is a steep learning curve to becoming a marketing expert. You will need to know the basics of the marketing process, from market research to making sales. Beyond this, you need to understand that the Net introduces a new note into marketing— interactivity. Buyers and sellers can communicate with each other any time, day or night. And sales information must let prospective customers point and click to find ever more product information, which is personalized to meet the needs of different customers. For example, some car buyers on the Net will be interested primarily in economy and gas mileage, while safety considerations will be foremost for others. It is also important that product information can be accessed in a reasonable period of time. Customers do not want to spend all their time waiting to see fancy graphic images slowly become visible.

Another important aspect of Internet marketing is knowing how to get publicity for your company's Web site so that shoppers will come and visit and, hopefully, buy. Just being part of a shopping mall won't do it as malls often have thousands of stores. Cybersurfers-turned-entrepreneurs must remember that some of the tried-and-true methods involving print, radio, and

TV work, as do newer methods associated with the Net. Here are a few suggestions:

- Advertise in computer and Internet magazines.

- Publicize your site to the media (you can use e-mail to do this).

- Register yourself in as many directories as possible.

- Cross-link your site with companies that complement yours.

- Advertise on welcome screens where users log onto a service.

- Get on mailing lists.

- Visit EPage's site at *http://ep/com/faq/webannounce.html* to discover online how to publicize your Web site in great detail.

You may be able to find a newsgroup that permits advertisement or a low-key mention of products or services. Caution: avoid "spamming," which is the inappropriate posting of advertisements. In other words, you should follow the rules of "Netiquette," which are the informal Net behavior rules. This includes avoiding the sending of unsolicited e-mail.

The books mentioned earlier in this chapter will give you a good idea of some of the fundamentals of marketing a product online successfully. Or you can go aboard the Net to read *NetMarketing*. It is available on publisher Michael Wolff & Company's Web site at *http://www.ypn.com*.

Step Four: Setting Up Your Internet Business

Like all businesses, setting up an Internet business is quite complicated. You will need a business plan that details what you are going to do and how you will do it. Fortunately, for cybersurfers interested in starting their own businesses, there is a gold mine of information on the Internet directed at helping you do business on the Net. You can spend time on the Internet while gathering valuable start-up information at these sites:

PARADESA MEDIA (*http://www.learnthenet.com*) tackles the question, "Can you make money doing business on the Internet?" in its "Doing Business" area. Solid advice on such things as understanding copyrights, getting professional advice, designing for different audiences, finding a site on the World Wide Web for a business, and publicizing a site is featured in the "Web Publishing" area.

INC. MAGAZINE (*http://www.inc.com*) offers information from over five thousand articles dating back to 1987, which you can access by searching by company name, management topic, or industry. There are interactive worksheets to teach you more ways to be smart about business as well as software for you to download and use in your business. Besides recommending sites for finding specific legal information, government agencies, and more, the "Reference Desk" area lists hundreds of books, videos, banks, Web developers, and newsgroups.

THE NATIONAL FEDERATION OF INDEPENDENT BUSINESS (*http://www.nfibonline.com*) offers free telecommunications and insurance guides as well as online workshops in such areas as starting a business.

U.S. Small Business Administration   (*http://www. sbaonline.sba.gov*) has such areas of interest as starting, financing, and expanding your business. It also features a shareware library of programs to run a business in its "Download" area.

Idea Cafe: The Small Business Channel   (*http://www. ideacafe.com*) offers a fun approach to serious business and at the same time has handy information on financing for aspiring entrepreneurs. In the "Financing Sources" area, there is information on borrowing money, getting investors, and learning about other sources of money. The "Getting Ready for Money" area includes: What kind of financing is right for you? (self-exam) and How much do you need? (budget sheet)

U.S. Business Advisor   (*http://www.business.gov*) exists to provide business with one-stop access to federal government information, services, and transactions. The goal is to make the relationship between business and government more productive. Here you will find a zip code lookup service, an overview of the W-2 filing process, forms and publications from the IRS, and other tools, guides, and forms to help you solve problems and do business with the government.

Step Five: Creating the Home Page

The home page, also called Web site, can be thought of as your cyberstore. It's the online spot where you present your product or products in text, graphics, and possibly sound and video. It isn't just one page but as many pages as are needed to fully describe your product or products. Customers can move from page to page using hypertext links that allow them to find the information they want.

Having interesting and well-designed pages is important to your sales success. The material on your pages has to be converted to HTML (HyperText Markup Language), the programming language that must be used so Web computers can read your material. If you lack the expertise to convert files to the HTML format or do not have sufficient design experience to create attractive pages, you may wish to hire a page designer or consultant. Chapter 5 describes the services these individuals offer.

Finally, before placing your home page on the Net, try it out. Make sure that every element works. You don't want your customers to discover that nothing happens when they click on a particular item. Also, ask other people associated with your business effort to check out your page. Look especially for confusing instructions or information.

Step Six: Opening Your Online Business

Once your home page is created, you are ready to open your cyberstore. Of course, you will need a computer and modem to access the Internet unless you elect to have someone else operate your business. You are most likely to access the Net through an Internet service provider. Chapter 2 describes the many marketing and technical services that ISPs offer.

You can get your store on the Internet in several ways. Commercial online services will put you on the Net as well as maintain the hardware, software, and security for your cyberstore. This is probably the least expensive way to get into business. Another option is leasing a space in a cybermall. Besides hosting your site and providing similar services to commercial online services, these malls will usually advertise the mall stores, run promotions to attract people to the mall, and may handle credit card transactions. In addition, some will help in the design of your home page. It is also possible to connect directly to the Internet, but this is a very expensive option that is best for large companies.

Learning Firsthand about Doing Business on the Internet

There is no shortage of information about doing business on the Internet in computer and Internet magazines and books and on the Internet itself. However, to help you understand what is truly involved in becoming an Internet entrepreneur, here are the stories of several individuals who are business successes on the Net. Only one of these businesspeople is an Internet guru. All, however, are savvy marketers who see the Internet playing an important role in selling products.

A Purveyor of Quality Web Resources

Thomas Boutell, a programmer by profession, can be considered a World Wide Web pioneer. Back in late 1992 when there was hardly a Web and no Web browsers for common PCs, he produced the first nontechnical magazine on the World Wide Web just for fun. Then during 1993 and 1994, he enjoyed maintaining the World Wide Web List of Frequently Asked Questions (FAQ). His skill in handling FAQs built his reputation, and Thomas discovered that what he'd been doing for fun was in demand. So he decided to take control of his own time and quit his job to write a book, *CGI Programming in C and Perl*, and expand his World Wide Web efforts into a full-time endeavor. The advance for the book gave him the opportunity to work on creating new programs dealing with the design of Web sites.

The new software was placed on the Net as shareware (free software for which users are expected to pay a registration fee).

Gradually, Thomas realized that he had a business as more and more money began to come in from registration of the shareware. His wife, who has also worked in the software industry, joined him in this endeavor and took charge of the financial side of the business, which was incorporated properly in 1995 as Boutell.Com. By 1996, the firm really took off, and his company became a Net business success story.

Today, you will find Thomas spending most of his time programming. Surprisingly, for a programmer, his workday is close to the typical corporate nine-to-five hours. His workplace and the company headquarters are in his home. From time to time, he answers technical support calls, which gives him a close look at what customers think of his product. Looking into the future, Thomas sees himself spending a major part of his time upgrading software to keep his customers satisfied as well as writing another book.

Thomas is president, his wife is the treasurer, and his sister is the office manager handling the day-to-day operation of the company. She was hired in 1996 to answer the phone, take orders, serve as customer service representative, and maintain the database because the business had grown so rapidly. The other employee is a software developer who works half time.

Although Thomas is a skilled programmer, he hired contract graphic designers to create his Web pages. He also uses them when he needs icons and product logos. He chooses to hire this work out because he wants quality graphics on his pages that will download in a reasonable amount of time. His advice to fledgling entrepreneurs is to be sure to bring an accountant into the picture at the start of any business enterprise.

A Closer Look at This Net Business

Boutell.Com is in the business of selling software that primarily deals with designing Web sites and gathering statistics on the number of people visiting a Web site. Thomas is the major writer of this software, which is mostly purchased by Web designers. From the home page, prospective customers can access a description of the company's many programs and then select those they would like to learn more about. When customers wish to look at or purchase a product, they can download it to their computers immediately. The registration fee for using the software is then sent to the company by phone, fax, or mail. If customers do not pay the fee and receive a certain code from the company, the software just stops working in thirty days. Sales of this software are evenly divided between phone, Internet, and mail orders.

Besides being able to acquire software, Net visitors to Boutell.Com are offered access to three other categories: Web information, entertainment, and activism information. Two of the information features offered are the extremely helpful World Wide Web FAQ (Frequently Asked Questions) and a moderated Usenet newsgroup. In entertainment, one of your choices is to post your birthdate and e-mail address so friends can send you electronic birthday greetings as well as access the Cybercard company to send you a card. Accessing activism information brings you into contact with groups such as "The Northwest Women's Law Center, USA." These extra features serve to draw repeat visitors to the Web site. Other marketing efforts include advertising on other Web sites.

The Company's Ideals

Dedicated to the ideas of "voluntary simplicity" and responsible environmentalism, Boutell.Com is a nearly paperless office that recycles as much as possible, reuses many materials, and obtains much of its noncritical equipment from thrift stores and yard sales. The company donates 10 percent of its net after-tax profits to nonprofit and charitable organizations. To promote the company's ideals most directly, Boutell.Com provides discount prices on several software programs to users in nonprofit and educational organizations.

The Online Booksellers

Along with computer equipment, books are decidedly among
the most popular items consumers buy online. Books are being
sold in cyberstores whose only storefront is on the Net as well
as those that also have land-based operations. Internet stores
range in size from giants selling more than a million titles to
small niche stores offering just needlework books. Someday
every land-based bookstore will probably also have a store on
the Internet. A fierce battle for customers is beginning to rage
and is expected to continue as more and more land-based super chains come aboard the Net. In 1996, Barnes & Noble hired
a staff of fifty to establish an online business, demonstrating
how important it is for bookstores to have a presence on the
Net. The search for customers already extends beyond the
United States. Codys Books, a forty-year-old land-based bookstore in Berkeley, California, is placing ads in the yellow pages
in telephone books in Singapore and Japan to entice customers to its online store (*http://www.codysbooks.com/*).

Bookselling in cyberspace is far more personalized than it is
in many land-based bookstores. For example, Amazon.com, the
biggest online bookstore with more than one million titles, lets
customers sign up for personal notification, via e-mail, of the
publication dates of the new releases of their favorite authors.
And Codys Books introduces its staff to you on the Web site
and details how each one can provide special help for you, from
answering questions about general science books to finding the
perfect book for older children. In most cyberstores, customers and staff use e-mail to communicate with each other. It's a
return to the days when bookseller and customer shared a dialog about books.

Amazon.com—An Amazon-Sized Bookstore

Today, Amazon.com is considered a pioneer online bookstore,
and it has only been doing business since 1994. Founded by a

former Wall Street executive, Jeffrey P. Bezos, the company has received $10 million in investment from venture capitalists. In keeping with its namesake river, this online bookstore has more than five times as many titles as you'll find at even the largest land-based chain superstores and is steadily growing even larger. Visit the store at *http://www.amazon.com* to see the many special features offered readers including "The Book of the Day," the authors born on the date of your visit, the opportunity to win prizes, lists of prize-winning books and books applauded by critics and customers, and the ability to search for books by title, author, subject, and keyword.

Point and click on "Employment Opportunities" to discover the many positions available at Amazon.com in areas such as programming, customer service, systems administration, Web design, finance, public relations, database architecture, copywriting, and advertising. Do you have the skills for positions that interest you? If not, think about how you can get them. To give you an idea of what Amazon.com is looking for in employees, here are descriptions of two positions:

E-MAIL CUSTOMER SERVICE SPECIALISTS   We are seeking exceptionally bright, articulate, computer-literate applicants for our high-intensity e-mail customer service department. Requires fast, lucid writing skills, strong analytical ability, high energy, and mastery over a complex set of database tools. Minimum four-year degree; advanced degree a bonus. UNIX, SQL, Oracle familiarity are big pluses.

CATALOG SPECIALIST   Excellent communication skills and the ability to handle many tasks simultaneously are essential for this catalog department entry-level position. Tasks include managing correspondence with publishers, tracking down information, and interacting with all departments at Amazon.com. Knowledge of UNIX and Perl at a user level is useful. Background in desktop publishing or graphic arts production and scanning a plus.

Bookserve—The Success Story of Two Young Entrepreneurs

You do not need to invest millions to start a successful business on the Internet. Brothers Michael and David Mason, who are only in their twenties, started Bookserve (**http://www. bookserve.com**) in their family's garage with a stake of only $20,000. They are proof that young entrepreneurs willing to work hard, survive for a while without making any money, and commit totally to their business can succeed if they have a solid product idea.

Michael and David started thinking about establishing their own business when one was tired of his career as a political consultant and the other was about to graduate from college. They knew something about the book business as their father had worked in book distribution and also knew that it was possible to start an Internet business without too much money as you did not need a physical storefront. After much investigation and consideration of other ideas, the brothers decided to put the databases of one domestic and three international book distributors online and sell books to cybershoppers. Their business would be service driven—focused on getting books to customers as fast as possible. It would also be global as it would offer international books that are not readily accessible in the United States.

The development team was made up of the brothers and two programmers who were given a percentage of future sales for their work. The programmers created the search engine for the database as well as the back-end work on the Web site (what you don't see). Michael and David, who had only basic computer skills, learned sufficient programming skills to create most of the front end of the Web site (what you do see). They also made arrangements with the distributors and secured access to the Internet through a service provider.

Going Online with Their Business

In September 1995, the Mason brothers' business went online, and sales orders were actually received the very first day. The early months were very busy, with twelve-hour days and a lot of work on weekends because the two brothers were doing everything. They would pull orders from their Web site, place them with the distributor (three-fourths of a mile away), pick up the orders from the distributor, and package and ship the books the same day. They were also answering e-mail (as they believe it is very important to talk to their customers), updating their site, and handling their financial work. In addition, they were busy publicizing their business by contacting search engines as well as online businesses that might want to link with them. For example, they might contact (by e-mail) a popular woodworking site and explain that they had eighty woodworking books that the other site's customers might want to access. They did not publicize their site through any newsgroups. The brothers, however, discovered that word of mouth does work, with satisfied customers bringing in more customers.

Within eight months, their business was making enough money that Michael and David were able to start paying themselves. Then a little more than a year after the business went online, they hired two college students to work part-time handling e-mail and whatever else needed doing. In this small company, everybody has to do everything. As their business continued to grow, they also hired an employee to handle general management chores, including ordering supplies and working with shipping companies; a director of systems to update the Web site and work with publishers; and a director of operations to manage customer service, shipping, and ordering. The brothers serve as principals overseeing the business. With success, they have been able to cut back on their work hours and are no longer working on Sundays.

Looking at the Future

The brothers are concentrating on growing their business. Much of their profit is reinvested in technology. They are also searching for new markets for their products. They believe that they have been successful because of their firm commitment to establishing a business even when the going was tough.

Online Catalog Businesses

Catalog companies are just beginning to open stores on the Internet. This seems like a natural marriage between technology and sales. More and more Americans have increased their shopping by mail and phone, so online shopping should be an easy extension of this trend. Prospective entrepreneurs can get helpful information on establishing an online catalog by visiting the Catalog Site at *http://www.catalogsite.com*, which links to many other online catalogs. Here you can find out about such things as selling catalog products online, marketing a catalog, handling customer service, processing orders, and producing an online catalog. You will also learn that you must pay careful attention to one of the Internet's unique constraints—download time—and avoid placing too many images on a page.

The easiest way to learn more about the successful creation of an online catalog is to look at several. Be sure to look at the catalogs of such well-known companies as Lands' End (*http://www.landsend.com*), Spiegel (*http://spiegel.com*), and L. L. Bean (*http://www.llbean.com*). You can also find catalogs by using a search engine to find "online catalog."

Bears by the Sea

In 1992, Kitty Wilde and a partner launched a retail store in Pismo Beach, California, to sell collectible teddy bears. The store also sells such bear-related items as stamps, books, and jewelry as well as a few other animals. Then in 1995, Kitty brought Bears by the Sea online to complement the retail store. The idea was to generate more income as well as to funnel people into the store.

Kitty had prior experience in starting several businesses, so she knew the importance of creating a business plan before going online. However, she had no computer experience and didn't even own a computer. A Webmaster made a sample site in just twenty minutes, which truly impressed her. Then her partner, who had never set up a Web site before, worked with the Webmaster to create the equivalent of thirty hard-copy pages while Kitty decided what should be featured on the site. This initial Web site cost $1,200. The only other expenses were buying a laptop computer so she could handle the business anywhere and securing an Internet service provider that offered unlimited local access. Within two weeks of contacting the Webmaster, Bears by the Sea was online.

To draw attention to her online store, Kitty put her URL (Web site address) on business cards, magazine ads, handouts, and just about everywhere. She also made sure that her company was listed in the right search engines and directories. Soon people were calling and offering to pay for links to their sites, as Bears by the Sea was such a high-traffic site.

Today, Kitty, who has become computer literate, spends two to three hours a day in Net activities. Most of her time is spent answering e-mail, but she also has to process orders, answer questions from her online forum, and evaluate what items to feature on the Web site. Marketing is another ongoing responsibility, which involves looking at other sites and for new search engines as well as e-mailing other sites for possible links. All of her efforts have paid off: 25 percent or more of her sales are from online customers, and many new customers have visited her store because they saw the Web site.

Kitty stresses that young entrepreneurs who are going online need to be patient. Business does not suddenly take off. It takes three to six months to get established. She also points out that Net entrepreneurs must be willing to learn the technology. She believes the Internet is the future and finds it exciting to be a part of it. Kitty says that at first she didn't know all the opportunities the Internet offers. She has started an Internet marketing business, lectures on how to start Internet businesses, and gives private instruction on the Internet.

You can learn more about Bears by the Sea and its unique features at *http://www.callamer.com/bears/*. The site features product information, an online question-and-answer forum, an online poll for a favorite bear, a bear orphanage that allows collectors to put bears up for adoption (sell them), and a directory listing all the teddy bear stores throughout the world.

Are You Prepared to Become a Successful Online Entrepreneur?

Just as the forty-niners rushed to California to pan for gold, hundreds of entrepreneurs are rushing aboard the Internet each week. Will you be one of the entrepreneurs who discovers online gold? You have read the stories of several successful online entrepreneurs. Consider now if you are prepared to start a successful online business or use the Net to enhance the sale of an existing product:

1. You have chosen a product that is a good match with the demographics of online buyers.

2. You have an understanding of how to direct potential online customers to your Web site.

3. You understand how to use advertising in marketing your Web site.

4. You are willing to take the time to develop a solid business plan.

5. You understand how an attractive and appealing Web site is constructed.

6. You have a good general understanding of how the Internet works.

7. You know how to choose the right experts (financial, technical, marketing) to help you develop your business.

8. You understand that you must offer something beyond your product that brings online customers repeatedly to your site such as helpful information, contests, or advice.

9. You realize that once you get your cyberstore open it will need to be updated constantly.

10. You are willing to make a strong commitment of time and effort to your online business.

Who Is Making Money on the Internet?

What you sell on the Net determines to a great degree how profitable your Internet business will be. The most successful companies on the Internet are those selling software, possibly because this is one product that can be shipped "through the wires." Computer hardware and consumer electronics are big sellers, too. Music distribution sites are also meeting with considerable success. According to *Internet World* magazine, the top five sites are selling more than twenty-five thousand CDs each day. In addition, books and vacation/travel are among the top products sold on the Net. Some well-publicized specialty niche stores have also had considerable success.

Looking Ahead

At present, few online businesses are making their owners rich. One reason online sales are not booming is that very few cybersurfers have acquired the Net buying habit, except for a few products. Nevertheless, consumers throughout history have shown their willingness to embrace new technology and ways to handle transactions. And the number of potential Internet shoppers throughout the world continues to grow at an astounding rate. There is room for considerable expansion in the number of Internet shoppers in the United States, as only half of the 35 percent of American households with computers can now access the Net. More Internet users will become online consumers as security concerns are effectively addressed, early Internet stores become more attractive, the reliability of product delivery improves, store inventories broaden, and store sites become easier to find. If online retail sales grow to $10 billion by the year 2000, as predicted by several market researchers, many online entrepreneurs will become the proprietors of successful cyberstores, and many existing stores will have increased their revenues through an online presence. Internet commerce is destined to become an important part of retail sales.

CHAPTER NINE

More Internet Career Opportunities

*E*very day cybersurfers find more ways that they can have careers closely associated with the Internet. The list is growing at an astronomical rate because so many Net surfers are determining how to turn their obsession with cyberspace into full- or part-time jobs. Whenever you go aboard the Net, keep your eyes open for more career possibilities and be sure to research Net job trends. Here are several more careers that cybersurfers and other online types should explore.

Teaching Courses on Using the Internet

If you are an adept cybersurfer, you can smoothly hop aboard the Net and surf for the information you want or explore new territory. There are, however, a great number of people who have heard about the Internet but are clueless about how to use it. For these people, words such as *browser, search engine, modem,* and *domain* are a foreign language. In order to access the Internet, Net neophytes need instruction. At the same time, there are people who want to put material aboard the Internet but need instruction in more advanced areas such as designing Web pages, marketing Web sites, or working with HTML and Virtual Reality Modeling Language. Others simply want to know how to use the Net for researching, shopping, or socializing. Furthermore, an enormous number of students in recently wired schools will soon need to know how to use the Internet for educational purposes. Because the Internet is not static but constantly growing and changing, each evolution spawns a dozen other changes. For this reason alone, there will always be careers in teaching Internet skills.

People needing to know more about using the Internet typically acquire the requisite skills from reading books, hiring trainers, attending classes, or talking to knowledgeable users. Community colleges, university extension programs, public schools, professional training companies, computer stores, public libraries, and even many Web sites now offer a variety of Internet training classes and need instructors to teach these classes. Except for public school instructors, who need teacher certification, the major job qualification for Internet instructors is to have solid online and communication skills. If being an Internet instructor interests you, get your feet wet by serving as a volunteer in a library program designed to teach patrons about the Internet. Most Internet teaching jobs at the present time are part-time positions. Instructors may be paid by the courses they teach or the hours they work.

Personal Internet Instructor

You don't have to wait until you graduate from college or even high school to become an Internet instructor if you are an expert cybersurfer. Joshua Joseph Soros is just in seventh grade; however, he is already giving both adults and children lessons on using computers and surfing the Net. Although he is largely self-taught, Joshua did take some children's computer classes and worked with a neighbor who is a computer graphic designer. As he gained expertise, children and adults began asking him to teach them, so he started a business teaching computer classes to individual learners. His only advertising is word-of-mouth and a listing on the local ISP.

Today, Joshua enjoys teaching others how to surf the Net, whether they want to do research or just have fun. His students learn how to use the Internet to do such things as check their stocks, investigate the weather around the country, and reserve books at the local library. In the future, Joshua wants to extend his knowledge of computers by learning how to fix them because he believes that people need to know how the insides of computers work. He counsels people his age to experiment and have fun now on the Internet in order to prepare for future jobs associated with the Internet. Joshua plans to continue teaching his computer and Internet classes for a while and looks forward to enrolling in college in the future with the goal of becoming an attorney and possibly a politician.

A Public School Instructor

Dale Beasley teaches an HTML class to middle school students as part of an elective program. The students have in turn created their own Web pages, which are included in the school's Web site. Dale has his own color flatbed scanner at home, which he used to scan student pictures and art to upload to the school's Web page. You can see his students' work at ***http:// www.halcyon.com/dale/stphil.html***. The hardest thing about his job has been convincing the teachers and students to contribute items so their Web pages remain viable and current. On the other hand, he has enjoyed helping other teachers set up their own schools' Web pages, including one college instructor in Sydney, Australia.

Community College Workshop Teacher

Early in the Internet era, Lorrita Ford, a community college librarian, realized that the Net would be a useful tool for gathering and disseminating information. She learned how to navigate on the Net by reading books, attending workshops, and subscribing to several listservs (Internet mailing lists). In 1993, she began to teach formal workshops to faculty and staff members. Within a year, she created a formal one-unit Internet course and incorporated the Internet into traditional print and electronic research courses. In 1997 she began developing a three-unit course on information competency and literacy, which will include using the Internet. Internet classes are now part of the community college research skills curriculum.

More Online Teaching Opportunities

Browse around the Internet, and you will quickly discover that it is a regular schoolhouse, with courses offered in such subjects as photography, genealogy, Web page design, becoming a United States citizen, word processing, cooking, and writing a novel. These courses may just be for a single session or last for several weeks. Use a search engine to discover the many places where "online courses" are offered. Then stop by and visit a few sites and consider whether or not you might like to become an online teacher.

An AOL Instructor's Story

First and foremost, Blythe Camenson is an author whose true love is writing novels. She is also a director of the Fiction Writer's Connection and writes a bimonthly newsletter for the association and provides a critiquing service and advice for members. It is with this background that she approached the coordinator of AOL's Online Campus and asked about teaching online. She proposed a course called "How to Approach Editors and Agents," which fit in well with the campus' writing department, and was soon teaching the course online. Now two years later, she is also teaching "How to Write Winning Query Letters." A background in computers is not necessary to join

AOL's Online Campus, nor is a teaching degree or experience required, but it is important to have a good command of your subject area and the ability to communicate well in an online environment. It also helps if you are a fast and accurate typist.

At the AOL campus, classes are held in live sessions. Each student sits at home in front of his or her own computer and joins others in a live classroom. As instructor, Blythe lectures a little, holds question-and-answer sessions, brings guest speakers to class (such as agents and editors), and makes material available to students in AOL's online library. Even though each class is only two hours a week for four or six weeks, the number of hours spent outside the classroom are almost uncountable. Blythe has lessons to prepare, registrations to keep track of, material to upload to the library, and the bulletin board to monitor. Furthermore, instructors sign on early before class and stay on late after class. Blythe also spends a lot of time with e-mail both before and during each term. Potential students have questions about her courses, which involves sending them class and registration information. And current students also have questions and often need help downloading materials and even finding their way to class.

Right now, for most instructors, online education only offers part-time employment opportunities, just as any live classroom in adult education settings do. Blythe is paid for each student in her classes. She receives $15 per student for her four-week course and $21.25 per student for the six-week course. There are also eight-week and twelve-week classes that pay a little more. In addition, she enjoys free AOL membership. Word-of-mouth brings her new students each term, and there are always repeat students. But to get a good class size, she has to spend time promoting her course online.

Although compensation for her time is very low, Blythe works as an instructor because she loves being able to help new writers avoid costly mistakes and finds it exciting "meeting" people from all over the country. She has even had students from Europe attend her classes. One of the biggest benefits of online instruction to Blythe is being able to teach a course from her home.

Information Brokers—Internet Super Searchers

Being an information broker is a relatively new career, as are the tools that are now being used to handle a great part of this job—the Internet and online services. What information brokers do is gather information for clients, often businesses, from a wide variety of resources, for a fee. While print was once the major information resource for information brokers, they are now spending much of their time online using commercial database services, published resources on the Internet, e-mail, listservs, and newsgroups. Information brokers may be self-employed or work for companies offering research services in a variety of fields. Many have been trained as librarians. An excellent source of information about this profession is *The Information Broker's Handbook* by Sue Rugge and Alfred Glossbrenner. If you go to ***http://www.onlineinc.com/pempress /super/toc.html***, you will be able to access articles about the careers of several prominent information brokers from Reva Basch's book, *Secrets of the Super Net Searchers*.

An Information Broker's Career Story

Mary Ellen Bates is currently the proprietor and sole employee of a research and consulting business that she started in Washington, D.C., in 1991. Her business is finding information for businesspeople. Here are examples of some of the kinds of research she does:

- the impact of information technology on the global economy

- the outlook for the pre-fab housing industry in Europe and Japan

- recent high-tech developments in the grocery industry

- joint ventures in the "edutainment" field

As an information broker, Mary Ellen uses online databases and the Internet as well as such resources as trade associations and government agencies. While she has been using online research-type databases since 1979, she only started using the Internet in 1992, when she enrolled in a two-day introductory course because she was getting nowhere fast trying to teach herself how to use the Net. Today, she feels at home with the contents of the Internet and has developed a good sense of how valid the information is. She must understand the bias of every source.

A quick look at Mary Ellen's day will let you see that being an information broker is not a nine-to-five job. What she does from day to day really varies. She may spend two hours on e-mail and listservs as part of her marketing efforts and professional development. Another hour could be spend doing work for the Association of Independent Information Professionals (AIIP) as she is the president (1996–1997). Administrative work such as paying bills, filing, and reading the mail may also take an hour. Because about a quarter of her business is writing, she is likely to spend two hours writing articles about the information industry, book chapters, or documentation and training materials. Then three to four hours will be spent doing online research, using both the Internet and professional online services such as DIALOG or LEXIS-NEXIS.

A Deep-Sea Diver

Mary Ellen generally considers herself a deep-sea diver rather than a cybersurfer, as she usually searches for in-depth information rather than skimming the surface looking for the next wave. She goes to sites that she knows and trusts because she has found reliable information there before. For example, if Mary Ellen were to get a question about travel to Albania, she would go straight to the Department of State (*http://www.state.gov*) because she knows that the State Department keeps travelers' advisories there. She does, however, become a cybersurfer when she is doing patent research because she has to look all over the Net for any prior mention of a possible new invention.

To handle all of her work, Mary Ellen uses two PCs and a laptop. She puts all her "good sites" on her home page so that she has access to them anywhere, whether she is working at home, traveling, or doing an Internet training course at a client's site. You can see these sites at *http://www.access.digex.net/~mbates/deskbook.html*.

Much of Mary Ellen's effort to stay current with general trends in her profession—as well as to learn about new sites—is done online. She subscribes to several library/information professional listservs and reads all the Internet material in ONLINE and DATABASE. She also reads Seidman's *Online Insider* (*http://wwwtechweb.com*) and *Inter@ctive Week* (*http://www.zdnet.com/~intweek/*). To keep abreast of what is happening generally on the Internet, she reads such print sources as *Internet World*, *Web Week*, *Searcher*, and *Information Today*.

Before owning her own company, Mary Ellen, who has a master's degree in library and information science, worked as a law librarian and corporate library manager for about fifteen years. To learn even more about Mary Ellen's work and professional activities, visit her previously mentioned home page.

Career Advice

Mary Ellen believes that there will be a continuing need for information professionals as more and more people discover how difficult it is to access the information they want quickly. Besides taking courses in business because they will be running a business, she feels that one of the most helpful things prospective information brokers can do is to join the Association of Independent Information Professionals (*http://www.aiip.org*). Go to the AIIP site to find out about the many benefits, which include matching new members with more experienced members who will give them advice on how to grow their business.

Writing about the Internet

The recent explosion of writing about the Internet offers a great number of cybersurfers the opportunity to have careers as writers. Visit the computer section of a bookstore and you will quickly discover a great number of new books on the Internet. Especially popular are books on how to use the Internet and how to make money on the Internet. People aren't just finding out more about the Internet from books; a number of very new print magazines have emerged that focus entirely on the Internet, such as *Internet World* (*http://www.iw.com*), *NetGuide* (*http://www/netguidemag.com*), and *the net* (*http://www. thenet-usa.com*). Furthermore, existing computer magazines now have columns and articles on the Internet discussing just about every aspect of the Net, from Java to instant Internet access to Web marketing tips. You can learn more about Internet and computer magazines by going to their Web sites, where you'll be able to see online versions of the magazines. Be sure to visit the staff page to see what types of jobs are available at different magazines.

Writing is a competitive field in which experience counts. An excellent way to get this experience is by reviewing Web sites. This is one job that future writers can gain as reporters on high school, college, and community papers.

An Online Book Author

Through more than forty books, Alfred Glossbrenner has introduced literally hundreds of thousands of people to the wonders of computers in general and the Internet in particular. The hallmark of his work is an uncanny ability to explain high technology in a way that absolutely anyone can understand. His wife, Emily, who has nearly twenty years of experience in computers and marketing, has collaborated with him on numerous bestselling computer books.

Since graduating from Princeton University in 1972, Alfred has been a full-time freelance writer, editor, book packager, and magazine columnist. Prior to 1979 he had written five "how-to" sports books. But that year he encountered what was then called a "dedicated word processor." It turned out that the machine could not only produce text, it could also "go online," a feat that was quite rare at the time. After half an hour of exploring The Source, an early online service, Alfred was hooked forever.

In the years since, Alfred has written extensively about specific online systems, about "how to look it up online," and about the Internet and World Wide Web. He has also written extensively about shareware, DOS, Windows 3.1, and hard disk drives.

The Glossbrenners typically write a book in approximately four to six weeks, frequently putting in twelve- to fourteen-hour days. They adopt a "total immersion" approach that yields a book containing the most current information available at the time. There are exceptions, of course, but the typical computer book earns about $15,000 to $20,000 and has a fairly short shelf life (six to twelve months). So it's important to be able to turn books out quickly.

It's also important to be creative and resourceful in getting the word out about your books. You simply can't count on the publisher to do the marketing and promotion for you. Alfred is a frequent contributor to computer and online magazines, which generates extra income and helps to publicize his books.

He also encourages readers to contact him directly by including his phone and fax numbers as well as e-mail and land addresses in all his books and articles. Getting feedback from readers ("Your book changed my life!" "At last, a computer book I can understand!") is one of the great nonfinancial rewards of being a freelance writer. It also makes it possible for him to establish a direct relationship with his fans so that he can alert them to new titles as they are published. Alfred takes this one step further by maintaining an online catalog and order form for all his current books. Fans with access to e-mail can get the latest version by sending a simple e-mail message to *books@mailback.com*.

Working in Libraries in the Information Age

Rapid changes in technology have brought computers into libraries. Many libraries now offer patrons the opportunity to use the information sources available on the Internet, which means librarians have to be Net savvy. Part of a reference librarian's job has become cybersurfing—going aboard the Internet to evaluate search engines and content and look for good links. Librarians are also turning into Webmasters and Web site builders.

Library Automated Systems Manager's Job

Cindy Brittain is the automated systems manager for the Contra Costa County Library system of twenty-three libraries in Northern California. In her career, she has alternated between being a reference librarian, cataloger, and automation librarian in public and university libraries. At first her job as an automation librarian primarily involved the bar coding and cataloging of books and working with the automated checking in and out of materials. Then in 1994, the library system installed Net workstations in eight of the county libraries that allowed patrons to access the Internet. Today, all of the libraries in the system have home pages and offer access to the Net. Patrons can now peruse the library catalog from their own computers and even reserve books.

Cindy's job is to direct the automation staff of four in the operation of the library's computer network. She also oversees the purchasing and planning of automated services. In her job, she needs to understand technical issues from a management perspective. Her Internet skills are self-taught. She is not a true cybersurfer in this job as she only goes aboard the Net to evaluate library services and to use e-mail. She sees the Internet as changing the way libraries do business.

Working in Internet Jobs for the Government

At the local, state, and federal level, government agencies are jumping aboard the Internet to offer information and services to citizens. You can download tax forms, find out about licensing fees and zoning regulations, read the notes on city council meetings, communicate easily with public officials—including the U.S. president—by e-mail, and do more each day as an increasing number of government units come online. This activity creates a tremendous need for government employees as well as consultants who know their way around the Internet. You can find out about jobs with the federal government online at FedWorld: The U.S. Government Bulletin Board (**http://www.**

fedworld.gov/jobs.htm). For state and local government employment service agencies, you need to go to *http://www.piperinfo.com/piper/state/states.html*.

A Job with the U.S. Department of Education

All of Peter Kickbush's professional jobs have been with the U.S. Department of Education. His current job title is policy analyst; however, he spends 80 to 90 percent of his time using the Internet. Peter and his colleague Kirk Winters research, write, and edit a listserv called EDInfo, which produces two to three messages a week of recent Department of Education studies, publications, reports, and funding opportunities. He also contributes to the Department's Web site. Initially, he was responsible for HTML markup, but now he serves as a consultant to others within the Department who are contemplating putting their information online. Peter works with individuals who range from external Web site contract managers to internal education policy makers.

The greatest challenge in his job is keeping up—not just with the furious pace with which new technologies hit the market but with the needs of the Department's customers and with modifying the systems to meet these needs. Peter believes that the Internet is redefining how the government interacts with citizens, and he finds it exciting to be part of shaping this redefinition.

Working in Net Jobs for Newspapers and Magazines

With the advent of the World Wide Web, hundreds of companies went online to create Web newspapers and magazines.

Unfortunately, they soon discovered that there was a very limited amount of Web advertising dollars, an increasing number of competing publishers, and subscribers unwilling to pay for content because they were accustomed to free Web pages. Overblown expectations have caused several publications to stop publishing or to scale back on their content. Most experts, however, believe that there are viable business opportunities for publications on the Internet in the future but that publications must be patient, wait for advertising revenues and cybersurfers' interest to rise, and find a niche with dedicated readers.

Online Newspapers

The newspaper subscription success story on the Internet is the *Wall Street Journal Interactive Edition*, which had more than fifty thousand paying subscribers early in 1997. Other newspapers, however, are finding that they can only charge for their electronic back files. Although the immediate future is not rosy, more and more newspapers are gaining an online presence, so there are job opportunities.

Senior Online Editor for Mercury Central

After working for trade publications and the San Jose *Business Journal*, Donna Yanish went to work for the San Jose *Mercury News*. She came to the newspaper as a copyeditor and worked on all copy desks for each of the newspaper sections. When Mercury Center, an online extension of the newspaper, started in May of 1993 as a site on America Online, she was asked to be one of the first two copyeditors. Her job evolved as the service evolved, and Donna is now senior online editor leading the content team for the *Mercury News'* Web site, which was launched in 1994.

The text of the daily paper posts automatically each day. The Mercury Center staff, along with some editors in the *Mercury News* newsroom, enhance a selection of stories each day with hyperlinks, photos, graphics, supplemental material, and audio and visual clips. It is Donna's job to lead the team of five online editors and a multimedia editor in that work. She works directly with each of the news departments in the paper to find out what they are working on and then chooses what is going to be enhanced with Web-specific elements. She does some researching for the hyperlinks, but most are supplied by the reporters, who know the material, or by the online editors she assigns to work on the stories that day.

Career Advice from Donna

The base of a job in online publishing for a news organization is good news-gathering skills. This is a relatively new medium, but as with the older media, content is key. Young people interested in online publishing should use the medium—and other news outlets as well. Read, watch, and listen to all you can online. Embrace the Internet as well as the other news outlets. Journalism school is a great way to learn news-gathering techniques and develop good news judgment. Schools are beginning to teach specifics for online publishing.

iWORLD—the Newspaper for Internet Information

iWORLD, located at *http://www.iworld.com*, is a daily online newspaper for Internet information and resources. Tristan Louis, who was named director of development of the newspaper in September 1995, only graduated from college in 1993, demonstrating the opportunities that exist for talented young cybersurfers. The managing editor directs an editorial staff of four full-time writers and twelve to fifteen columnists who write area-specific columns once a week on special topics such as Java specialty technologies. These writers are journalists. Rounding out the small staff of this online-only publication are two ad salespeople who sell banner ads, a marketing person who markets advertising, a director of development charged with seeing that the newspaper is positioned properly technologically, and five artists and HTML programmers who format and put the publication online. The general manager of the Web site, Chris Elwell, oversees the editorial, sales, marketing, and technical staffs.

Online-Only News Organizations

Newspapers, magazines, and radio and TV networks are not the only news sources on the Internet. The Web is loaded with sites promising to bring you the latest news. CNET, at **http://www. news.com**, is a twenty-four-hour-a-day technology news service covering the computer industry and the Internet. In addition to providing about twenty-five original stories every day, the site offers links to interesting stories in other publications, weekly columns by some of the editors, and interviews of leading technology figures. The more than thirty editors and reporters on the news staff are mostly experienced journalists from newspapers and magazines. Go to the Web site to see how the news is presented and for job information. Other news services include: CMP's TechWire at **http://www.techWeb.com/ wire.html** and Microsoft's venture with NBC at **http://www. msnbc.com**.

News Editor at NEWS.COM

You don't wait for the presses to stop when you are news editor at NEWS.COM (**http://www.news.com**) as it is a twenty-four-hour-a-day technology news service aimed at PC users. Clair

Whitmer, the news editor, works from 8:30 A.M. to 7:00 P.M. or later assigning stories, making sure deadlines are met, and editing stories. It is essential for Clair and her staff to work as quickly as possible to meet the day's three main deadlines, which require the posting of three to twelve new stories. Handling this job requires Clair to be on the Internet throughout the day checking competitor's sites, doing research, and looking at the NEWS.COM site.

Online Magazines

Since the first days of the Internet, there have been magazines, called *zines*, on the Net. Most zines are published by individuals and don't usually carry ads. There are as many as fifty thousand zines on the Internet. Now major print magazine publishers, online services, and start-ups are trying to get magazines online. One of the best-known Web launch efforts is Microsoft's *Slate*. It is an interactive magazine of politics, policy, and culture edited by Michael Kingsley, who is the former cohost of CNN's *Crossfire*. Because of the reluctance of subscribers to pay for online publications, there will be no fee for *Slate*. Online magazines employ a staff that is similar to that of online newspapers. If the magazine is associated with a print publication, the editorial staff is primarily involved in adding Web enhancements to articles. However, staff on a publication that is only online will have the responsibility of creating original copy, as would the staff of print publications.

Senior Editor of *the net*

Pat Joseph first started using the Internet for research; now he is a true cybersurfer spending most of his time online in his job as senior editor at *the net* magazine (**http://www/thenet-usa.**

com). *The net* is published bimonthly, and a part of the magazine is placed on the magazine's Web site. Pat is in charge of the magazines's "blue pages" (actually printed on recycled blue paper), which form a comprehensive guide to the best of the Web. You can read the blue pages online as well as in the magazine.

In each issue, more than 250 sites are reviewed—from the arts, politics, gaming, zines, and sports to the truly bizarre—and Pat spends a great part of his day surfing the Net and looking at new sites before he chooses the sites to be reviewed. He writes a few reviews; however, most are assigned to twelve freelancers who write short reviews of one hundred words and long reviews of four hundred to five hundred words. This is an excellent first job for writers and pays from $.10 to $1.00 per word, depending on the magazine.

As editor Pat also has the responsibility of editing all the reviews, finding new reviewers, and spacing out the deadlines. While his job keeps him very busy, he has found it to be more fun than he ever imagined. It truly sounds like a perfect job for a cybersurfer.

GolfWeb—A Different Way to Hit the Links

This Web site is for golf aficionados who want golf stories, tour coverage, statistics about golfers and golf courses, audio interviews with professional players, instructional pages, and golf chat. It is an extremely popular site, receiving more than one million hits a day with traffic growing 20 percent a month. GolfWeb has a staff of approximately thirty employees, including writers, marketing people, and engineers. The staff also works with about forty correspondents around the world, and the site has two versions—English and Japanese.

Editor of GolfWeb

Stu Schneider, a ten-year veteran with *Golf Digest* magazine, works sixty hours a week as editor of GolfWeb. Much of that time he is directly working on the Web site, as he is responsible for all the content on the site. The biggest challenge of his job is to make sure that the information on the site is constantly updated and correct. The company is on a twenty-four-hour publishing cycle, and with readers all over the world there is no such thing as a deadline. As readers in the United States are going to bed, readers in Japan are just waking up. What Stu likes best about GolfWeb is its immediacy. Unlike most other media, online companies can update information within minutes.

While Stu says the biggest job market on the Internet right now is for technical people, he believes that will change eventually as the Web tools and technology become easier and easier to work with. Then he believes that people with an editorial background will become more and more valuable.

Your Internet or Online Job Can Change

Many cybersurfers and online types have found that their jobs have evolved organically in this fast-paced information revolution because new opportunities are constantly appearing. Reva Basch, who has been associated with online activities since the early 1980s, is an excellent example of how careers can evolve. She began her online career, long before the advent of the Web, as a researcher at a pioneering independent research company where she really learned to use online research services, such as DIALOG and LEXIS-NEXIS, and ended up as the company's vice president and director of research. Her next move was to the technical side in 1986, when she went to work for Mead Data Central (now LEXIS-NEXIS) designing front-end software for the NEXIS search service. Then in 1988, she started her own firm, Aubergine Information Services, which provided online research on just about any topic. Her business has evolved over the years; at this point, she does very little research but a lot of writing and consulting to the online industry.

Seventy-five percent of Reva's time is now spent writing. She has written three books and now writes a monthly column called "The Cybernaut" for *Computer Life* magazine in which she talks about anything that has to do with going online, finding information, or socializing with other people online. She also wrote a bimonthly column, "The Compleat Searcher," for *Online User* magazine that focused on strategies for finding information online, in both commercial services and on the Net. In addition, she contributes feature articles to *Computer Life* and other magazines such as *PC Novice*, *Link-Up*, and *Focus*. Her consulting activities take the remainder of Reva's time. She works primarily with companies in the information business doing such things as helping them design better and more useable databases and online services.

Reva works alone and at home, frequently putting in ten- to twelve-hour days and working on weekends. She is online for most of the workday—sometimes she keeps her Net connection up all day because she is always going online and off. After work this online aficionado goes online to socialize, and she always travels with a laptop. You can learn more about Reva's career and life by visiting her home page at ***http://www.well.com/ user/reva***.

Other Job Areas to Explore

So many jobs now have a tie-in with the Internet. Doctors and lawyers research on the Net and consult with each other through newsgroups and e-mail. Tax preparers find forms on the Net and even file returns online. A minister downloads a sermon from the Internet to use with his congregation. Thousands of company employees work from home using the Internet to reach their companies. Fast-food and take-out restaurant workers receive orders over the Internet. All advertising and marketing people now have to consider the Net in the promotion and sales of products. In the future, you can expect most jobs to have some association with the Net—great news for cybersurfers and other online types.

CHAPTER TEN

Looking at a Bright Future

Without question, cybersurfers and other online types, you are in the very early days of a communications revolution that will have a tremendous impact on lives, jobs, and companies—an impact that we haven't really begun to feel. On the horizon, as more and more people come aboard the Internet and its capabilities increase, the vision is emerging of a world where you can communicate with anyone, anywhere, at any time, and even see and hear that person. It's a world where millions of bits of information will be literally at your fingertips. And it's a world with video-on-demand, online shopping and education, digital documents replacing paper documents, news delivered interactively, low-overhead electronic banks, virtual-reality (three-dimensional) "worlds" that you can explore, and more than you can ever imagine. The Internet hasn't even scratched the surface of its potential.

This communications revolution is moving so fast that the Internet is different every few months. You are in the midst of historic change. At the same time, as a cybersurfer who is fascinated by the Net, you have the opportunity to contribute to the evolution of the Internet through the career you select. Improved technology is needed. You could be one of the many who will find technical breakthroughs. Business and professional people and educators who understand the new technology and want to use it in the workplace, homes, and schools are needed. You could be one of the many to bring the Internet into people's lives and workplaces.

Predicting the future is always difficult. Surprises inevitably occur. Nevertheless, it should be helpful for cybersurfers beginning to plan their Net careers to see what prominent players in the cyberworld think about where job opportunities and the Internet will be in the next few years.

Bill Gates—Chairman and CEO of Microsoft Corporation

In his book, *The Road Ahead*, Bill Gates made the Internet his central focus, just as virtually everything that Microsoft is doing these days is focused in one way or another on the Internet. Here are some of his views from the book on the impact of the Internet on jobs as well as career advice for cybersurfers:

Lots of companies will eventually be far smaller because using the Internet will make it easy to find and work with outside resources. Within the next ten years, we'll start to see shifts in how and where we work, the companies we work for, and the places we choose to live. My advice is to get to know these empowering new technologies as best you can. The more you know about them, the less disconcerting—and the more helpful—they will be. Technology's role is to provide flexibility and efficiency, and your goal should be to take advantage of it.

From The Road Ahead *by Bill Gates. Copyright © 1995 by William H. Gates III. Used by permission of Viking Penguin, a division of Penguin Books USA Inc.*

John Levine—Author of *The Internet for Dummies*

Well, there's a flash in the pan of Web site builders, but I expect that to shake out in a year or two. In the longer term, as the Net goes more and more mainstream, I expect that the biggest job growth will be in training and support for Internet users, particularly business users.

There'll also be a lot of work building and maintaining Intranets, particularly intracompany Web sites, where the work is mostly getting the material organized and presentable, rather than any fancy programming.

Margaret Riley—Net Consultant and Creator of *The Riley Guide*

One thing to note is that when I began doing my work on the Internet, it was still in relative infancy compared to what it is now. I am self-taught and learned on the job. Today, that's not good enough. You have to have credentials. The world is finally waking up to the fact that the programmers are not the best information managers, so more librarians and editors are taking over the content of the Web servers. However, you must have demonstrated experience in this area, and building your own home page isn't enough any more. I have an entire university Web server behind me and my own site and my reputation as someone who can divide the good from the bad. I built that over the last three to four years.

Peter Kickbush—Policy Analyst, U.S. Department of Education

I've never been very good at predicting, but in the future, I think jobs on the Internet will be hard to discern. Everyone will be using it for everything. So my advice to young people would be to diversify yourself. Without a doubt, double major in college—one major in computer science or engineering, the other in business or the humanities. Take logic and philosophy courses. Learn about the technology, but don't be seduced by the notion that technology in and of itself is the answer. Think of technology and the Internet as the vessel that carries information. I think people who will successfully exploit the overwhelming potential of the Internet are those who understand both the vessel and the information. Individuals who use this incredible tool to communicate meaningful information and ideas will find jobs on the Internet.

Reva Basch—Cybernaut Columnist, Book Author, Net Consultant

From a librarian's perspective, the Internet desperately needs better indexes and search tools. Beyond that, I'll just say that the Web, or whatever it evolves into, is going to be the platform for information and communication into the foreseeable future, and the possibilities are virtually unlimited.

Egil Juliussen—President of Computer Industry Almanac

Eventually, the Internet will emulate all present-day communications functions. In the distribution of information, the Net will have the capability of the telephone, radio, television, newspapers, and magazines. Plus it will add many new functions. At the present time, the Internet is rather like a vast library with all its books on the floor. Individuals will be needed in library-type jobs to bring order to this chaos or the Internet will not live up to its potential.

Keeping Up with What's Happening on the Internet

Dedicated cybersurfers and other online types, your passion for the Internet is what will keep you informed about changes on the Net that could affect your career. As you become more and more knowledgeable about the Internet, bookmark those sites that offer solid information about what is happening on the Internet so that you can easily visit them again and again. Visit the home pages of Internet magazines and newspapers frequently to look for career and technology information. Check what is happening at companies like Microsoft and Netscape—leading players in the Internet world. Everything that you need to know about choosing an Internet or online career is on the Internet. Enjoy your cybersurfing!

Glossary

ARPANET   The forerunner of the Internet, developed by the Department of Defense in the late sixties and early seventies.

ASCII   American Standard for Computer Information Exchange. Plain text characters that can be read by almost any program. Pronounced "ask-key."

Applets   Small downloadable Java applications that can be run from a Web page.

Backbone   A high-speed line that forms a major pathway within a network or links one complete network with another.

Bandwidth   A measure of the amount of information you can send through a connection.

Baud   The speed at which modems transfer data, listed in BPS, or bytes per second, or kbps, or kilobytes per second.

Browser   Software used to surf the Web.

CGI   Common Gateway Interface, a programming language used by most Web servers for handling forms.

CTI   Computer Telephony Integration, the convergence of computer and telephone technologies.

Cybermall   A collection of business Web pages offered online by one Web access provider, often anchored by a major store. With advances in encryption, cybermalls are increasingly able to offer direct purchases over the Internet.

Domain Name   A unique name identifying an Internet site.

Download   Copy a file from a remote system to your computer.

E-mail   Electronic mail, it is both a noun and a verb.

Ethernet   A common way to connect computers in a LAN (Local Area Network).

Encryption   Scrambling a message so that it is difficult or impossible for another person to read.

Firewall   A method used to protect a network from access by those outside the network.

FTP   File Transfer Protocol, a system allowing files to be transferred from one computer to another via the Internet.

Gopher   A tool for finding and retrieving files on the Internet.

Home page   The main page out of a collection of Web pages, it is also used to mean individual's or businesses' own Web site.

HTML   HyperText Markup Language, a formatting language used on the World Wide Web that allows links to be made with other WWW documents.

HTTP   HyperText Transfer Protocol, a standardized set of rules for passing Hypertext documents on the Web.

Hub A network connecting device linking computers, printers, and other devices.

Hypertext A type of document containing links to other documents.

Internet The group of interconnected networks using TCP/IP protocols.

Internet Telephony A service that allows you to make long-distance telephone calls over the Internet.

InterNIC Internet Network Information Center, a data and directory service funded by the government. Domain names are registered with InterNIC.

ISDN Integrated Services Digital Network, offering digital data transfer speeds of either 64 BPS or 128 BPS over regular phone lines.

ISP Internet Service Provider.

Java A programming language using small Java programs called applets that can include functions such as animation.

LAN Local Area Network, a network linking computers and other devices within a small geographic area.

Mailing lists Also known as discussion lists or listservs. An automated system that allows people to send e-mail to one address that automatically copies and re-mails the message to everyone who has subscribed to that particular list.

MMX Multimedia extensions, allows PCs to deliver images quicker and in more TV-like fashion.

Modem A device that allows computers to talk to other computers over the phone lines.

NAP National Access Provider.

NAPs Network Access Points, where the backbones connect and exchange information.

NSP National Service Provider or National Backbone Operator.

Netiquette Internet code of behavior.

Packet A group of bytes traveling between hosts on the Internet. They may be of variable length and contain a variety of user information, but all contain information about where they came from and where they are going.

PC Personal Computer.

POP Point of Presence, a location where a network can be connected.

POTS Plain Old Telephone Service.

PPP Point-to-Point Protocol, a fast, reliable method of connecting computers on the Internet.

Protocol A set of rules used to define communications between computers.

Router A networking device that uses software to examine packets of information to decide which path should be used to send information to its destination.

Server A computer or software package providing a specific service to software running on other computers.

Site   A specific set of pages on the Internet.

Snail mail   Mail sent by the U.S. Postal Service as opposed to the nearly instant e-mail.

Spamming   Posting of inappropriate commercial messages on newsgroups.

Streaming   The processes of downloading and using a data file before the full file has been received.

Switch   A simple version of a router that uses hardware to direct traffic at high speeds.

Surf   To randomly search for information in the hopes of finding something new.

T1   A digital phone line used for high-speed data transmission. It offers the fastest speed commonly used to connect networks to the Internet.

T3   The high speed lines often called backbones which are used to link networks.

TCP/IP   Transfer Control Protocol/Internet Protocol, standardized sets of computer guidelines that allow different computers to talk to each other.

URL   Uniform Resource Locator, a type of address that points to a specific site on the World Wide Web.

vBNS   Very high-speed Backbone Network System; the scientists' network.

VRML   Virtual Reality Modeling Language, a language used to display three-dimensional information on the screen.

WAN   Wide Area Network, a network of computers spread out over a great distance.

WWW   World Wide Web, a hypertext and hypermedia system. Also, the resources that can be accessed using Gopher, FTP, HTTP and other tools.